Bread and Roses, Too

Eleanor Wolfe Hoomes

Eleanor Hoomes

PublishAmerica
Baltimore

First printing

At the specific preference of the author, PublishAmerica allowed this work to remain exactly as the author intended, verbatim, without editorial input.

ISBN: 1-4137-8321-X
PUBLISHED BY PUBLISHAMERICA, LLLP
www.publishamerica.com
Baltimore

Printed in the United States of America

FOR VICTORIA ROSE JORDAN

Acknowledgements

I wish to thank the following people:

Larry Johnson and Sharon Hearnburg for reading the manuscript of BREAD AND ROSES, TOO when it was two-thirds written and encouraging me to continue writing poetry, Dianne Cox and Claire Baker for reading the manuscript when it was completed and making suggestions for improvement, the West Georgia Writers Guild for encouraging me to continue writing, and my husband, Wendell Hoomes, for all of his help and encouragement.

SECTION ONE

ELIZABETH: BREAD AND ROSES, TOO

In 1912 in Massachusetts
Women factory workers,
Exhausted by inhuman working conditions,
Outraged by starvation wages,
Unladylike, went on strike.
Made bold by the justice of their mission,
Potent in their solidarity,
Seeing with clarity their dismal future,
Enraged, they demanded a living wage.

Rallying one another,
Relying on each other,
Undeterred, united in sisterhood,
Strident, they hurled their words
At an indifferent world.
Demanding to be heard,
Insisting their demands be granted,
    "We want bread and roses, too."
United, as one, they chanted,
    "We want bread and roses, too."

What is it that I want today?
Forget what I say about feminist issues,
What women are due,
What I value and hold true.
It's simple, I argue, nothing new,
What I want is
    "Bread and roses, too."

ELIZABETH: ROLES

How many personas
Can I house in one soul?
Do I bend and sway,
Displaying situational identities,
A different identity
For each scene played during the day?

How many people should I be today?
How many different roles should I play?
Who should I be this minute, this second?
        A daughter, a wife,
        A mother, a sister,
        A gardener, a cook,
        A car pool driver,
        A follower, a leader,
        Victim or survivor?
        A shaker, a mover,
        Secretary or boss,
        A winner or a loser
        In the cosmic coin toss?
        Should my mask be
        Comic or tragic,
        Upbeat or down,
        Puzzled or angry,
        A sneer or a frown?
        Should I display a self-negating,
        Ingratiating,
        SMILE?

Should I try to please,
Die to please?
How should I respond?

Which should it be?
Which face should the world see?
Today, this minute, this second,
Sisters, what should my role be?

CHARITY: I WANT TO DANCE

I want to dance,
To express joy in motion,
To fling my limbs about,
To snap my fingers, kick,
Clap, stomp, and shout.

My father and his god
For girls and women decree
Long hair and long skirts,
Prohibit make-up and TV,
Forbid dancing.

I want to dance,
To swing and sway,
To twirl and whirl,
To leap through the air,
To defy gravity.

My father and his god
Forbid dancing.
Dancing, they say, is a sin,
An open invitation
For the devil to move in.

I want to dance,
To express joy in living,
To fling my limbs about,
To swing, to sway
Without fear and trembling.

I do not understand
My father's definition of sin.

Unacquainted with the devil,
I would never invite him in.
I just want to dance.

ABBY: THE LATE COMMUTER

I join the mechanical river,
Destination— Atlanta,
Swept south by the current of flowing traffic,
One pressurized worker per tin can,
Impatient, late, pushed for time.
Got to get to work on time.
       Move over, you moron,
       Get out of my way,
       Slow traffic to the right—
       Where do you idiots come from, anyway?
Sixty, seventy, eighty—
Flowing along, making good time.
Going to get to work on time.
Pulsating blue, yellow, red—
High-pitched wailing ricocheting in my head—
       Accident on I-75 snarls morning traffic,
Shout the gleeful deejays.
       Expect delays.
The south flowing current jams,
Stopped by a late commuter.

Isolated, insulated in my private tin can,
I drum my fingers on the steering wheel,
Staring straight ahead,
Cursing the delay.
An elongated tin can,
With measured cadence,
Bereft of pulsating red,
Removes the cause of the delay.
The blockage cleared away,
The mechanical river trickles, flows,
Sixty, seventy, eighty—

Dare I push it to eighty-nine?
Got to make up that delay.
Got to get to work on time.

ABBY: DREAMS

waking to my world of disarray
full of bustle and cacophony
mind as untidy as my unmade bed
impeccably groomed and arrayed
can't take time for a bit to eat
got to get that Lexus on the street
got to sell my soul in the marketplace
to greedy eyes and dollar hearts
demands of career stretching me taut
as a rattler about to strike—

dreaming a world of otherness
      an azure world of circus tents
      cheering crowds
      and I in a cerise leotard
      of sequins and beads
      flying with reaching arms
      from trapeze to trapeze

SERENA: FOREVER SMILING

Forever smiling a smile
That cannot unsmile itself,
A sepia salutation, locked in a silver heart,
Captivated by your phantom smile, I am
Forever hostage to your smiling charm.

You died young, my smiling mother,
Who should have walked in grace, in beauty,
Enduring unto the end, prevailing.
You died young, my smiling mother,
Teaching me early
That most things break.

You died young, my wavering mother,
Unable to see through the obscuring darkness
Blanketing the window squares of your hermitage.
You died young, my wavering mother,
Teaching me early
That nothing lasts forever.

You died young, my treasonous mother,
Embracing Death with welcoming arms,
Choosing Death over me.
You died young, my treasonous mother,
Teaching me early
That love is never enough.

Were you unaware, my smiling mother,
When you capitulated,
Shutting tight the valves of love,
That death vanquishes love,
And that death is forever?

LEE: FUGITIVE

Refusing to give
Refusing to take
How many towns did she leave
        miles did she drive
        hearts did she break
Avoiding winter?

Searching for summer dreams
In cumulous white
Slipping away in the dead of night
A fugitive
One step ahead
Of the long arm of love.

Her traveling companion
        unbreachable solitude
No losses restored—
No sorrows ended—

ISABELLE: SLOW LEARNER

A charming lady once said to me:
    Wisdom and truth are not learned from a seer.
I don't believe she made that up.
To me it's clear
    she likes to speak in negative absolutes.

Another companion, pragmatic, precise, volunteered:
    Wisdom and truth are the comb and brush
    Life gives you after you have lost your hair.
Now, I know she got that from Dear Abby.
She just changed a word or two here and there.

A gentleman friend, somewhat perverse, replied:
    What piffle.
(Did I mention that he is also persnickety?)
    Nature is a perennial philanderer,
    Sowing seeds of truth and wisdom randomly.
I'm not sure what he meant,
    but it had such a nice sound,
    and others thought it profound.

I prudently held my tongue
    because by then I had discerned
    that for me
    truth and wisdom will always be
    just beyond the periphery
    of my next birthday.

MARILYN: BLONDE

Subsumed by blondness,
     Circumscribed,
     Defined,
Having more fun,
Desiring to live her life
Only as a blonde.

With a sub-rosa chemical alliance
Repelling the attacks
Of the advancing roots of darkness,
Captive in the Land of the Lightness
Of Counterfeit Blondness,
     Forever young,
     Forever blonde.

COURTNEY: WIRED

wired
plugged into sterile electric currents
flickering graphics her hearth
e-mail her family
chat rooms her village
blind windows her face to the world
bolting out light//shutting in dark
imprisoned by wires of electronic connections
pervasive//invasive
electronic isolation her passion//her art
kept alive by alternating impulses
plugged in~
connected & wired passive
@home.com

JACKIE: IF I COULD REWIND TIME

If I could rewind time—
Change actions of his and mine—

Would I choose the man,
            uncleaving,
Attend the party,
            where the man betraying
Immersed his guilts in brut champagne
            while sampling his host's wife
            in her lush pantry?

Would I pull my righteous disdain
            tight about me,
Leaving him to exchange
            the arms of his host's wife
For the welcoming arms
            of the one surviving
            elm tree on Jackknife?

Unshriven, unforgiven—
On Jackknife the elm tree
            terminating his contract with life,
            with time, with me.
Time— mine—
            inexorable, linear, advancing—
There are no rewind buttons in real time.

REBA: EARLY ALZHEIMER'S

standing on the edge
                    of my
                    mother's
                    days
          INADEQUATE
I watch her life
                    draining
                              away
like water swirling
                    down
                         a drain
depleting her personhood
her brain rotting like stinking cabbage
left too long in the rain
her life pieced together like a crazy
                                   quilt
with jagged bits and torn
                              pieces
of barely remembered
failures   indignities   betrayals
successes   loves   dreams
forming a pattern barely perceived
through shifting mists of memory
her mind a sieve
                    leak
                         ing
all connections with her past
indiscriminately
                    leak
                         ing
love   relationships   language
          IMPOTENT

21

I watch her relentless
her irreversible advance
toward imprisoning freedom

TRACY: TEMPTATION

Beautiful as Apollo, he was,
Standing amid his seductive flames,
Smiling, beckoning to her, who
      won on playing fields and courts,
      parasailed from cliffs, rode waves,
      sailed to exotic ports.

Beautiful as Adonis, he was,
Standing amid his greedy blazes,
Pledging eternal pleasure to her, who
      captured that elusive butterfly,
      scaled mountains, hiked trails,
      surfed the clouds in the sky.

Beautiful as Achilles, he was,
Standing in his flaring radiance,
Swearing endless ecstasy to her, who
      believing, ravenous with desire,
      in a chilling fever,
      walked into his alluring fire.

Irresistible he is, a satyr,
Stepping from his tempting fire,
Looking beyond her, now reduced to
      a bit of bone and a hint of hair,
      enslaved by freezing passions,
      solitary in his burning snare.

SHARI: THE NAME OF THE GAME

She says Shari is her name,
Love the name of her game.
Her game has many other
      names as well.

Veiling body from soul,
Bereft of kisses, eyes closed,
Pungent odors of bought sex oozing
      from her pores.

Exiled in a revolving door
Where all partners are named John,
Empty-eyed shadow men
      with masked faces.

Vampires drunk on anonymity,
Rubber legged, flaccid,
All vanquished by the unmasking
      light of day.

In the unveiling morning light,
Bereft of kisses, eyes opaque,
She washes and scrubs,
      washes and scrubs—

Purifying.
Sanitizing.
Baptizing.

SHANNON: MULTIPLE CHOICE

What would she trade for wealth and fame?
Her good left hand?
Her respectable name?

A bullet to the thigh?
Twenty points of I.Q.?
Her good right eye?

Wit's bitter delights?
An early trip to the grave?
Five inches of height?

Life without love?
Her answer is:
Any— or all of the above.

MATILDA: THE ARTIST

I painted pretty pictures,
Never painting anything disturbing,
Anything perturbing,
Faithfully reproducing what my eyes saw.
           Oh, they look just like photographs,
Said viewers who came to see,
Believing they were praising me.
My technique was superb,
All within a realistic paradigm.
Careful, meticulous strokes,
Capturing a fleeting look, a gesture,
Copying nature, freezing it in time,
Lovely to look at, pleasing to see,
Lacking passion, lacking vision,
Insipid and empty.
I was a copyist wanting to see,
Searching hard to become
           an artist.

Dissatisfied,
I turned a painting on its side
And then upside down.
My vision cleared as I looked inside,
Pulled into the core of seeing,
Where a hanging lamp
Silhouetted against a silver shed
Became the back of a woman's head,
Shadowy, mysterious,
Full of unknown fires, hidden desires,
Resolving into a story
That haunts, disturbs, perturbs.

Painting what might be there,
What could be true,
Seeing more than the eye beholds,
Guessing at what the soul knows,
I was finally an artist
in the process of becoming.

JOANNA: IF ONLY

"A done deal," he assured me,
With a toothy grin,
Back in the early 1980's.
"A win-win situation for all—
The investment of a lifetime,
Guaranteed not to fail."
And so—I uncapped my pen,
And cleaning out my bank account,
I began to write Check #110.

"What was that stock again?"
I asked as I finished writing the check.
"Home Depot," he replied,
Reaching eagerly for the check,
As I recapped my pen.

The rest is history,
So they say,
And it would have been,
Had I not, after careful consideration,
That very same day,
Rescinded the buy order,
And voided Check #110.

SARAH ROSE: RELIGIOUS BIGOT

My god is a personal god,
Created in my own image.
I am his chosen messenger.
He speaks directly to me
Telling me how you
Should live your life.

TANYA: SOLITAIRE

Between the tangled, sweat-soaked sheets—
     that substitute for passion,
     that animal instinct,
     that urge to procreate—
Triple methods thwarting the creation of life,
     preventing contagion—
Sans the shorthand of familiarity
     non-lovers,
     non-mates.
Khaki souls kept apart
     even as bodies strive to connect
     through triple barriers—
Spent.
Evasive opaque hearts avoiding shifting eyes
     while retracting promising lies
     whispered in the heat of animal passion—
Finished.
Silently retreating in beige shadows
     he to his den
     she to her lair
Both decorated in taupe shades of solitaire.

ROSE MARIE: COVER THE MIRRORS

Something innate in her loved a mirror—
That courted and seduced in yellow light
The reverse image in every mirror encountered,
While reflecting indifference to other lovers.

Like Narcissus,
        drunk on captivating impressions of Self,
Youthful radiance emblazing desire,
Attracting and returning Self-love,
Self-esteem bloated
        with the pleasure of her reflected visage,
Imprisoned by her infatuation
        with her mirrored image.

Peeling through the layers of her days,
Shedding the corset of her infatuation,
Peering into the suppressed mirrors of her heart
And seeing her likeness turned inside out,
Her aging elegance stripped bare,
        revealing her true essence
Like murky night reflections
        from darkened windowpanes.

Repelled at the images revealed,
Passion for Self ashy memories,
Calm, lifeless as the mirrors
She once loved and now fears,
        "Cover all the mirrors," a whispered sigh.
Then persistent, insistent, commanding,
        "Cover all the mirrors so I can die."

MONA: MONSTERS

with no invitation, without even knocking
Five Monsters moved into my brain
DARKNESS hardening like stone
PANIC buzzing like a swarm of angry bees
TERROR attacking, blocking reason
PAIN warping reality
FEAR gobbling up sanity
brain a full boarding house
time, action, logical thought evicted

frantic, desperate
seeking relief
embracing the alchemy of black velvet
the suspension of time
filling my head
with images of bulldozing irrational fears
phobic reactions
out the backdoor of my mind

until the Monsters
darkness, panic, terror, pain, and fear
all five
vacated the premises
evicted by a bulldozer driven at full throttle

my head again my own
I now reside there
        lonely
        alone

BONNIE: CONFESSIONS OF A DEDICATED SHOPPER

She has dedicated herself to shopping.
Her mission in life is praying for bargains,
Buying and charging.

Market research proves that if she wants it,
She'll buy the stuff she doesn't need
And won't use,
Hurrying to get it while it's still hot,
Because tomorrow it'll be worthless junk
Thrown onto an overflowing waste dump.
She purchases status symbols,
Brands herself with labels
To confirm her identity,
Help fill the empty spaces.
She purchases the lifestyles
Of the rich and the famous,
The youth and beauty of professional models,
Who tempt her with their promises of wealth,
Fame, youth, beauty, and eternal health.
Her life has meaning and she belongs
Because she buys;
She owns.

Succumbing to the temptation of easy access,
Worshiping in the Temple of Excess,
Kneeling at the Altar of Materialism,
The mall her church,
E-commerce her creed,
Consecrated to consumerism,
Baptized in greed.

Buying and consuming—

For life without end—
Forever and ever—
      Amen.

NITA: PINK SLIP BLUES

Expected, dreaded, but still a shock,
Once again that monster pink slip
In my salary packet
Causing my stomach to drop.
    Cut back, downsized,
    Laid off, let go,
    Reorganized—
    A pink slip still means I'm fired.

Little money in my pocket,
Even less in the bank,
Where will I get the cash
To pay the overdue bills
And fill the gas-guzzler's tank?
The severance pay will barely cover
The rent money due today.
VISA and MasterCard maxed out,
Child support in arrears,
And the kids have hands outstretched
For lunch money and new shoes.
Send out the revised resumes,
Dust and press the navy blues,
Interview, wait for the phone to ring.
    Cut back, downsized,
    Laid off, let go,
    Reorganized—
    A pink slip still means I'm fired.

How can I feed my kids when
The president of the company
Got a million dollar bonus,
But their struggling, single mama

Has been downsized again?
Cut back, downsized,
Laid off, let go,
Reorganized—
A pink slip still means I'm fired again,
A pink slip still means I'm fired.

PATTI: THREE PACKS A DAY

She has an appointment with Death—
Smoking three packs a day,
She moves closer with every puff, every breath.

He's waiting just around the corner,
Impatiently tapping his fingers against the lamp post,
A cigarette dangling from his mocking lips.

Smoke lazily curling toward the light,
Hazy green eyes hidden behind mirrored shades,
Anticipating the strike of midnight.

She senses he's waiting there,
Just around the corner,
Anticipating her imminent arrival.

She thinks she can cross the street,
Travel a different path—
Lighting the next cigarette from the last.

NICOLE: THE RULES

Hungry for a husband,
She is like a cat,
Crouched, ready to pounce,
Tail slowly twitching,
Attentive, seductive,
Elusive, calculating.
Eyes tracking every male movement,
Tracking the prey, tracking the prey—
Stalking, stalking, stalking—
Sensing weakness,
Leaping—
The stunned prey—
Captured and tamed.

PAMELA: SUMMER DANCE

once
for a light-filled summer
she had been happy

now when she hears laughter
she sometimes remembers
that she was once young
and danced with Johnny
and was happy for a summer

then came the green-eyed brunette
smiling, crooking her finger
tempting Johnny
and Johnny fled
without apology
without good-bye
to the brunette's narrow bed

once
for a dance-filled summer
there had been laughter
before the twin conquerors
time and chance
heralded the onset of winter

FERN: ANNIVERSARY

A hot wind blowing across rolling hills,
Rippling the heat of a humid July night,
A brick mini-mansion in a gated neighborhood,
Diamonds dripping on close-shaved grass
From brilliant sprinkles arching to and fro
At 129 South Wood Row.

Celebrating a rare night together, sans children,
Happily recalling where and how and when
They fell in love. And then—
Forbidden words escaping—
Disturbing the smooth flow of the celebration,
Igniting flares of anger,
Fanning stockpiled irritations, worries, fears.
The one voted most likely to succeed
Hurling hoarded resentments
At the former homecoming queen,
Now bombarding him
With her own catalogue of disappointments,
Anger fanning rage,
Fueled by profuse infusions of celebratory wine.
Close to hand a family protector, loaded, primed,
Easy to reach, easy to aim, easy to fire—
Bang! Surprise! You're dead!
And so she is—
Trice pierced through the heart,
Only one shot needed to stop its beat,
To betray its love, to steal its future.

Instant sobriety, instant remorse,
Yes, but— murdered wives accept no apologies.
Grasping the finality of death,

Aiming the family protector—
Loaded, primed—at himself,
Death's impetuous emissary,
In three minutes creating two orphans
While the diamonds arched to and fro
At 129 South Wood Row
On the sixteenth wedding anniversary
Of the former homecoming queen
And the one voted most likely to succeed.

KATHARINE: THE JOURNALIST

Long and lean, with
Elegant bones, fiery-hearted,
Projecting charm and candor
With a face the cameras adore—

A tourist in her own life,
Portraying herself as a living legend
Striding the earth
Independent as the wind—

Cloaked in shifting fashion,
Hostage to daily deadlines,
Advancing her career with
The world's troubles and fears—

Writing truth, her version,
Editing facts to fit her vision,
Speculating, adding a dash of fiction,
Even when the truth would suffice—

JONI: CARTOGRAPHY OF A FRIENDSHIP

You reproach me for coldness,
Reprimand me for remoteness,
Accuse me of masquerades,
      camouflaged by charming smiles.
You say I circumnavigate our friendship,
      sailing around the borders,
That you can't locate the
      center of my being,
That when you come searching
      you never find me home.

You don't need a compass.
You've already discovered
      and charted the native me.
I can always be looked for and found
Precisely where I've been
      and where I am,
At home, emotionally situated,
      on a thin line stretched taut
      from the frozen North Pole,
      to the ice-bound South.

My Dear, I am what I am.

AMY: CRISIS MODE

Existing in crisis mode,
Dramatizing every episode,
Relationships imploding—
Events exploding—

Playing dual roles
Of terrorist and victim,
She is the producer,
The director, the playwright
Of her daily dramas,
The actor, center stage,
In the spotlight.
If, by chance,
Her life should start going right,
She'll break an arm,
Crash her car,
Lose her job,
Goad her best friend into a fight—
Emotions in overload—

Ready to implode, explode—
To keep her life in crisis mode.

ARIEL (LEGALLY CHANGED FROM ALICE): SUCCESS

She wanted wealth
And with strategic planning
And tactical maneuvering she sought it,
Finding her fortune
In paradoxes and contraries,
Circumventing her honor, she bought it.

She wanted fame
And with a master marketing plan
And illusions of candor she sought it,
Finding her celebrity
In reverses and converses,
Evading her integrity, she bought it.

She wanted love
And with a targeted audience,
And a mission statement she sought it,
Looking for adoration
In inversions and inventions,
Forfeiting the truth, she bought it.

Now striding the apex of her life,
She weighs investment against gain
And dares to ask herself:
Was the climb to the top
Worth the price, worth the pain?

My God, yes!
She is quick to explain:
How else could I have lived?
What else could I have done?
In a heartbeat, I'd do it again.

SHARON: WISHING

She wished the encounter
Could turn into loving,

She wished the loving
Would last all night,

She wished the night
Would last all summer,

She wished the summer
Would never end.

LEAH: POACHING

Poaching on her Sisters' Preserves,
Seeking fleeting reprieves from boredom,
Hunting for husbands not hers,
Unconcerned about lives disconnected.

A predator, lured by the forbidden—
The stimulation of the chase and
The thrill of the capture
Feeding the adrenaline-starved demons within.

Releasing to their wives and children
Mangled prey too easily trapped.
Publicly exhibiting the best specimens,
Flaunting trophies of hard-won victories.

Dissatisfied, terrified,
Each safari less gratifying than the last.
Her hunting license permanently stamped:
      Happiness denied.

GINA: PAYMENT

Forever hostage to a youthful decision
       and to the disappointment of those
       not finding their delight
       in another's misfortune—

Hungry for past happiness—
       before the sins of neglect and doubt,
       before the death of desire and vanity,
       before the alluring words soon forgotten
           by the whisperer,
       but forever haunting, taunting
           the listener—

In the supermarket of her imagination
       she makes her selections,
       consulting the tightly clutched shopping list
       and checking off each item she chooses,
           memories distilled of moonlight
           and purified by time and distance,
           wrapped in golden pastels
           that never existed—

Paying with a life time of regrets
       for the parcels of her life wrapped in
       last year's grease spotted newspapers.

OLIVIA: EQUATION

Her past frozen in the ice of the present,
Unable to conjure the memory of love or desire
From that part of memory excised by the surgeon,
Who removed the monster consuming her brain
While releasing her from opaque pain.

Time could not rebalance the equation of love,
Of contagious togetherness and the bliss
Of flying while keeping their feet on the ground.
Time could not restore vanished passion,
Veiled beyond any recall of present memory.

Encased in eternal ice—love exchanged for life,
She could only watch through translucent pain
The split of the equation,
The slow silent death of his love
No longer balanced by her love in return.

GWEN: THE TRAVELER

I was born with itchy feet,
With a compelling compulsion to explore,
Always wanting to learn more, more, more
       about what was around the next bend,
       over the next hill,
       across the next body of water.
Exotic places, exciting places tempted me—
       come and see,
       explore me.
For me the only thing better than coming home
       was leaving again.
My favorite place—always the next one.
By the time I was forty,
       I had lived and worked
       and traveled the world over.

Then one day the only thing better than leaving home
       was coming back again.
One morning I awoke with no place left to go.
No place beckoned me, tempted me—
       come and see,
       explore me.

Now, my daughter, like her mother
       was born to wander,
With a need to discover
       what is around the next corner,
       over the next hill,
       across the next body of water.
Far away places, exotic places tempted her—
       come and see,
       explore me.

She did not resist,
Nor could I insist that she stay home
When it was her time to travel alone.

CHARLOTTE: THIRTY DEGREES OF WHITE

White—her world—white—
No brown for her, no black,
No rainbow hues—
Insulated day and night
In thirty degrees of white—
  christening dresses,
  tennis frocks,
  gardenia corsages,
  wedding gowns,
  friends,
  white brick walls,
  shrouds—
Cloaking herself in her own white lies,
White anger at invading hues,
Like ice cubes
Splintering into sharp needles,
White wine fueling white-hot passions,
Igniting her fears, her hates—
Incarcerated behind
Locked white wrought iron gates,
Hostage to her blind tribal pride,
Three hundred and thirty degrees
Shut outside,
Confined day and night,
Isolated in her world
Of thirty degrees of white.

While her God's in her Heaven,
All's white in her world.

JANENE: TOMORROW

living to break the rules,
loving to break her heart,
internal combustions fueling
       her manias,
       her depressions.

caught in a perpetual whirlwind
       of panic and recovery,
teetering between the pain of reality
       and the relief of denial,
using outrageous humor
       to hide suicidal despair,
gray-colored lenses
       covering her eyes,
abetting her belief
       in self-defeating lies.

tomorrow—
monday—
the first of next month—
for sure the first day of january—
the new beginning of a life
       lived with order,
       lived with responsibility,
       lived with joy.

unable to face the daily routine
       of living without illusions—
slipping back into the whirlpool
       of dark humor,
plunging back into the
       ebony

gossamer
of
delusions.

EVELENE: WORKING WOMAN

As naked as the newborn babe,
I walk through the jungle, so afraid,
Terrified of shadows, sudden noises,
Furtive movements, pungent odors,
Whistling
       Won't you come home Bill Bailey,
       Won't you come home,
       I moan the whole night long—
Abruptly changing the tune to
       Put on a happy face.
Head held high, shoulders straight,
Eyes alert for predators—
If just one, a lion, per chance,
Ever sensed my fear, I'm sure he'd pounce.
But if I bluff and hide my fear,
Possibly, just possibly—
That stalking lion won't come too near.
But if he should—
Oh, what the hell—
I'll just extend my hand.
After he sniffs it and smells it,
He'll either lick it,
Or eat it,
Or perhaps—
Perhaps he'll shake it.

REBECCA: CONTRACT

She found a man to save her—
To lead her from darkness into light,
From confusion to understanding,
From chaos to order,
From desolation to fulfillment,
From poverty to wealth.

A bargain was struck,
A contract signed in blood—
All He asked was her soul in return.

ANNA: AN AVERAGE DAUGHTER

My name is Anna;
I'm here to confess:
My daughter Jana is average
In looks, talent, intellect,
Mediocre, at best.

She is one of the pack
With no desire to be top dog.
Waiting, weighing, standing back,
Never the first to take the lead
Nor the first to succeed.

I wanted a daughter who excelled,
Who would stampede,
Who would break glass ceilings
That stalled me in my tracks.
I wanted bragging rights.

That little sapling
Doesn't grow far from this tree,
I now know that
When I describe my Jana—
I am also describing me.

LOUISE: A FATE WORSE THAN DEATH

It was as if, Athena-like, she sprang full grown
From a Greyhound bus one bitter January morning,
A leather suitcase in her left hand,
A battered briefcase in the right,
An alligator purse pressed between upper arm and side,
Wearing a coat too light for the cold.
The next day there she was—
The new owner of Louise's Cafe,
With its high tin ceiling and
Age-darkened oak beams.

She didn't wear her name well.
The name she gave the town, Louise Smith,
Somehow seemed borrowed,
Put on temporarily just for us.
When pressed, she said she'd lived all over
And had no family left.

Tall, willowy, jet-black hair, green eyes—
Beautifully mysterious—
We each wove our own fantasies about her,
Making her impossibly superior.
She was always smilingly gracious,
Speaking to everyone by name,
But an impervious shield surrounded her
As she moved through town.

Four years later
When a handsome stranger came to town,
Asking questions about Louise Smith,
I led him to Louise's Cafe.

But when we broke open
The locked door to Louise's Cafe,
Above the kicked over bar stool,
We saw
Louise Smith's slender high-arched feet
Twisting, twisting—

VERNAJEAN: FLICKERING REALITIES

Telling the story of hair burned black,
Eyebrows singed, third degree burns
From her recent decent into hell and her climb back—
    (Interrupted by messages selling, selling)

Into the concealing shadows
She walks alone,
Scuffling for clues in dead ashes—
    (Interrupted by news flashes breaking, breaking)

Mysterious, tall, dark, handsome lover
And elusive beauty, secret agents who discover
Intrigue and happiness under cover—
    (Violin music building, breaking)

Her life an empty house, its deed hidden,
Her mother's house destroyed, its hearth exposed,
Her father's house ghost-ridden—
    (Steel guitars humming, strumming)

Black helmets hiding,
Black leather gloves, jackets, boots, riding,
Menace on motorcycles roaring, gliding, sliding—
    (Bugles blowing, drums beating, soaring, soaring)

Last scene: conflicts resolved, motives revealed,
Lovers reunited, high body count, all ending well,
Remote aimed, trigger finger flexed for what's coming on next—
    (Tension-building music swelling, swelling)

In a subterranean room, blinds drawn, unseen,
Silently huddled around a flickering machine,

Measuring universal realities on a room-sized screen—
(The End. Credits rolling, scrolling)

JOLENE: CEASE FIRE

"If you loved me," she sniffed,
"I wouldn't have to tell you.
You'd know."
She waited,
Saying nothing in a pointed fashion,
Speaking volumes without words.

Silence.
He reclined on the sofa
In his habitual laconic pose,
Facing the fire, mute,
Relishing the silence.
Then with a burst of taciturnity,
He asked, "How?"

She swiped at nonexistent tears.
"You just would," she retorted.
"If you loved me, you'd know."
They sat, wrapped in the loud hush.

"What am I thinking now?"
His asking shattered the quiet.

"How the Hell should I know?
Oh-h—," she giggled.
Then with a soft purr
She snuggled into his open arms,
Male and female intertwined
On the sofa facing the fire.

For one brief voiceless moment,
Muddled by desire,

Two spluttering minds—
And bodies—
Cease fire.

DONDRA: I CANNOT HATE HIM NOW

I cannot hate him now
Though love is dead,
Slain by candle wax
Dripping like molten lead
When flickering flames
Revealed feet that were not
The feet of a true lover.

I cannot hate him now
Because I loved him then,
My passion an elastic promise
Stretched hard edged and golden
Before tarnishing and snapping.
I inhaled his vows.
They sizzled through my veins,
Colliding hot licks of love and lust.
I basked in his beauty,
While pondering the mystery
Of his long and narrow,
His elegant leather shod feet.

I cannot hate him now
Though love is dead.
Like Psyche my obsession grew,
And I plotted,
Plotted to uncover
That which was hidden
From me by my lover.
Betraying him into drugged slumber,
By leaded candle light
I unlaced fine leather
To discover

Not the long and narrow
Elegant feet of Cupid,
But the cloven hooves of Pan.

ASHLEY: DREAM LOVER

I wanted a man captivated by my charms,
Who would find me irresistible,
Huggable, kissable, snugable, beddable,
Make my toes curl and my hair tingle,
Kindle fires, incite desires, virile,
Sexy, sensual, passionate, sensational,
With a sense of humor, whimsical,
A little comical, congenial,
With a sense of proportion,
A companion interacting on all levels,
Physically, emotionally, intellectually,
A dreamer of dreams,
Capable of flights of fancy,
Wealthy, tall, and handsome,
In the chin a simple dimple,
A charming smile, flirty eyes,
I wanted a marvel of manhood,
Someone worthy of my devotion,
Who would love me above all others,
Steadfast with a sense of reality,
Romantic, idealistic, full of vitality,
Committed to me for all eternity.

I found this perfect lover,
Only to discover—
That it is heaven on earth
To love a dream lover.

JEANETTE: MY NOVEL

It's thick and fat,
Full of humor, grief, and strife,
Its characters true to life.
It enriches the soul and warms the heart
With its universal themes—
This novel I compose in my dreams.

It's prominently displayed in bookstores,
One of Oprah's Picks,
The December selection of the
Book of the Month Club AND the Literary Guild.
It's on all the Best Seller Lists,
Winning awards and critical acclaim.
Translated into fifty-four languages,
It's posted on the International Site
Of Books That Changed the Course of History—
This novel that I plan to write.

I'll start this classic masterpiece
After the youngest starts to school,
Or when my mother dies, so I can include
Explicit sex and four-letter words,
Or after the last child leaves home
And I make an office in his room,
Or after the grandchildren are grown.
Maybe after I retire or my husband dies,
I'll commit to paper all my notes,
For this novel that I never wrote.

DEIRDRE: THE FEMINIST

Standing toe-to-toe with brothers
       who mainlined
       essence of male chauvinism
       with mother's milk,
I fought for respect.
Slapped down for being an uppity female,
I rebounded,
       demanding a fair share of my world.

Fighting for equal opportunities,
Winning in the courts,
       losing on the playing fields,
Celebrating Roe vs. Wade,
       that hard won victory
       of a woman's right to choose,
Struggling for every inch gained,
Thankful for the first tokens
       but pressing for more,
Fighting for my daughter
       and my daughter's daughter,
Winning scattered battles
       but never the war.
Working to leave a legacy,
       a confederacy of
       liberated sisterhood.

My daughter, a Gen Xer,
       never votes,
And my granddaughter
       collects Barbies.

SHIRLEY: HIGH EXPECTATIONS

She never loses faith
That her knight will appear
And she will live happily ever after.
The next man will meet her expectations,
Will present her with adventure,
Fulfillment and order,
Will resolve for her forever
That mystifying equation
Between innocence and experience.

She never loses faith,
Drifting from one amorous disaster
To the next,
Discarding each successive romance
Because of expectations unmet.
Time and age bulk her body,
Fade her hair,
Add weariness while
She dreams of the perfect mate,
Always believing in the kindness
Of Capricious Fate.

She never loses faith
That her expectations will be met.
She revels in the initial euphoria
Of a promising new romance,
Just knowing in her heart that
This time she has found her savior,
Yet doomed to replicated failure.

DEBRA: THE MARRYING KIND

Darling, I'm just the marrying kind, I guess.
I fall in love so easily, but it never lasts.

Yes, that's right; I've had eight husbands,
Eight absolutely marvelous weddings,
None of them the same.
I just love weddings, don't you?

No, no, there were no children.

Of course, I remember each husband's name,
And all their faces, too, for all that.

Sure, I can name them.

In order? Well, then.
The first was Joseph, very tall, somewhat stiff,
But surprisingly full of fun and mischief.
You know, he's the only one who died.
If he had not—
Oh, well, that was a long time ago.

The second was William,
Full of wisdom, solemn, no problems.
Nevertheless, he soon grated on my nerves,
And I demanded my freedom.

The third, Douglas, the gorgeous Atlas,
Who too soon became a pompous jackass.

Number four, Thomas, the chivalrous,
At first scrumptiously luscious,

Then, bang—he became nervous, self-righteous,
And finally just simply obnoxious.

Langford the fifth,
Charles number six,
John seventh,
All three very much the same—
At first fascinating, but soon boring.
But, Darling, notice that
I do remember each one's name.

And the last, number eight, that was Edward.
Edward—mannered, cultured,
Be-whiskered, good- natured,
And then, that dastard developed
Into a self-centered drunkard.

Darling you want to know what goes wrong,
What happens?
Well, there's usually two years of blind passion
When I see no warts,
Followed by one to two years of disillusionment,
Of seeing ugly, disfiguring warts—
All sorts of warts,
More and more warts every day,
Mountains of warts tumbling all around me,
And I just have to get away.

What's that you say?
You think that you're wart free,
You want to be Number Nine?
Well, Darling, you're the fourth one this month,
So, take your place at the end of the line.

NEELE: MY HANDSOME YOUNG MAN

Where have you gone to,
My Handsome Young Man?
Far from our garden,
Our cottage, our plans.

Where have you gone to,
My Husband, my Mate?
Far from our bower,
Our marriage, our gate.

Where have you gone to,
My Sweetheart, my Lover?
Far from our children,
Their mother, our summer.

Why did you leave me,
My Heartsease, my Pride?
For a guilty shroud
And Death by my side.

Where have you gone to,
My Darling, my Other?
To my single grave,
Farewell, my ex-Lover.

When can I join you,
My Comfort, my Fate?
Never, I bide in Hell,
Heaven is your state.

PAULENE: ODE TO/ELEGY FOR CREDIT CARDS, WRITTEN IN CLICHES

VISA came courting, knocking on her door,
Uninvited, but nevertheless, welcome,
Offering to fulfill her dreams with easy credit.
She signed the plastic, called the toll-free number,
Accepting with alacrity VISA's marriage proposal.
Celebrating the union with a bottle of vintage wine,
Drunk in a toast to a union improving with time.

A new TV, a leather jacket, a diamond ring,
A previously-owned Chrysler convertible Sebring,
Living the American Dream of living within her means
Even if it means using plastic to achieve that dream.

Next MASTERCARD and DISCOVER knocked on her door,
"Come right on in," she invited. "There's room for two more."
Department stores and others became insatiable suitors,
And soon her wallet bulged with twenty-nine licenses to spend.
She was fair to her twenty-nine lovers, giving each one equal time—
Trips, furniture, dining out, an emerald ring,
A new Chrysler Sebring, more vintage wine.

Then the bills started to trickle in one at a time,
Expecting HER to pay for that first bottle of vintage wine,
Now triple its original price.
Borrowing from Peter trying to pay Paul,
Building a house of plastic cards, all,
Until a crash, a bang, a quake and a gigantic fall.
Then all the king's horses and all the king's men
Couldn't put her credit rating back together again.
All twenty-nine lovers promised her paradise in large print,
The small print she didn't read, much less bother to heed.

Now her new bumper sticker reads:
    I owe, I owe. It's off to work I go.
    Because I owe, I owe, I owe.

CHERYL: LIVE OAK

On the April morning when I was born,
Grandpa Hartsell dug up a sapling,
A live oak twenty inches high,
Just as tall as I,
And planted my birth tree in his back yard
Where I could see it from my cradle
        through the tall windows.

Today I stand less than six feet tall,
But my birth tree is 40 feet tall
And just as wide,
Reaching outward and upward,
Destined to die without ever touching
The sun, the sky, the clouds,
        or the horizon.

But flourishing in the kiss of the sun,
The smile of the sky,
The tears of the clouds,
The promise of the horizon.
Holding its world together
With tangled, anchoring roots—
        providing shelter and beauty.

Connecting me to my story,
To my birth, my earth,
        and to God's universe.

EDITH: THE TALKER

vandalizing Silence and Solitude
pelting Tranquility with
  a cloudburst of words
  a spate of premature confessions
    of infantile sins
rococo tongue traversing a dessert
  of inane braggings
inviting sympathy for pseudo travails
while invoking the name of God
words spilling, tripping, stomping
  on the heels of previous words
pugnacious words screaming, shoving
  fighting to be heard

stupefied non-listeners
envisioning vaporization by vanity
of using word strippers
on verbal veneers

a final barrage
a valedictory of verbosity

Tranquility returns
on hummingbird wings
hovers
sipping the Elixir of Silence
while Solitude once again sings

TONI: A REASON FOR LIVING

Thoughts of making an early departure
        keep her breathing.
Her leaving will be executed
        with style, with finesse.
She will swallow pills, of course,
        no damage to her beautiful body,
        a body made-up,
        manicured, pedicured, waxed,
        buffed, tinted and coifed.
She has honed her farewell epistle
        into a literary masterpiece,
        to be published posthumously
        amid excitement and critical acclaim.
Her going-away party, planned to the last flower,
        will be attended by the rich and famous
        and multitudes of her close friends,
        all publicly mourning her untimely leaving.
Her filmed and refilmed last will and testament,
        a stunning work of art
        rife with sound bytes and film clips,
        is ready for mass distribution.
Like Princess Diana's, her living and leaving
        will be extensively covered in
        international newspapers and magazines
        and on special marathon memorials on TV
        preempting regularly scheduled programming.
She has bought coordinated outfits for the event;
        they hang in her closet, unworn, waiting,
        a mini-history of fashion, but
        she can never resolve the quandary of shoes:
        to wear or not to wear
        remains an unanswered question.

Until she can solve the mystery of shoes—
  she'll continue to draw breath,
  secure in knowing
  that she always has the option
  of taking an early death.

SUSAN: TIME

She stumbles around in her brain
    shying away from bleeding memories
Then slides down to the edge of her heart
    sits on the rim, legs dangling over the side
    forcing herself to look inside
    afraid to leap into the past contained therein
Searching—
Searching—
    for lost faith
    for absolution
    for God
But God died in 1999
    when the ball rolled into the street—
        and froze time.

CLAIRE: LOVE SONG

I spent my youth singing off key,
Out of tune with others around me.
Alone in my otherness,
Failing to harmonize, to force
My voice into an accepted range,
    Low notes out of my reach.

Despite all efforts, I sang off key—
Out of tune with others around me.
Atonal.
There was music in my heart,
But I was without
    The voice to express it.

I met you, a singer as atonal as I,
The high notes out of your reach.
We joined our solo voices in duet,
Blending each with the other,
Finding our voices complementary
    When we sang our songs.

Singing our words to our own tunes,
Releasing the music in our hearts,
Songs dancing between the two of us,
Music soaring,
Setting our souls free, as
    We sing our lives in harmony.

NINA: GREENER GRASS

Seduced by illusions
Of greener green, and
Motivated by greed,
I deluded myself into
Thinking that the grass
Was, indeed, greener on
The other side of the fence.
Convinced of my discontent,
I hanged myself because
Of some undefined need
By sticking my head through
The black wrought iron fence
To taste, to feed
On grass on the other side
Growing in the same soil
And from the same seed.

CLAIRE: GREENER GRASS

Seduced by promises
Of greener green, and
Besieged by yearning need,
I broke through the fence
To taste the greener grass
Growing on the other side.
Greedy with hunger,
I tasted, I grazed, I feasted,
Dancing, reveling, gorging,
Basking in the perfume
Of forbidden greener green,
Lush, succulent, aromatic
Waves of greener green
Satiating my starved senses
As I awakened to
The empowering freedom
Of breaking through black
Wrought iron fences.

ALICE ANN: THE SMILER

Mama, you told me,
     SMILE.
You pinched my little girl face up into a smile.
You spent thousands of dollars on orthodontia,
So my perfect teeth would shine in a smile,
Blind in a smile.
Mama, you told me,
     Smile and the world smiles with you.
     Listen and smile,
     Smile through your sadness and pain,
     Always smile and you'll get your man.

I got my man, Mama.
He was a good provider,
Just as you promised he'd be.
He supported me in style.
You could brag to your bridge club
About your daughter who married so well.

But, Mama, he just left me,
Left me for a smiling champion smiler,
A ten-year younger model of me.

I sat there smiling, Mama,
While he told me he was leaving.
But, Mama, what I need to know is—
Mama, can I stop smiling now?

HELEN: THE GARDENER

Spring.
Rebirth.
Persephone returns to her mother, Demeter.
Released by Pluto,
She returns from Hades to the surface of the earth,
Regenerating from the darkness
Underneath the surface of the earth.

I emerge after an angry winter.
I have shaken my fist in God's face,
Ranted and raved,
Cried and raged at a silent God.
Like Demeter when she first lost Persephone,
I am demented.
But unlike Demeter,
Who knows Persephone will return to her each spring,
I know I will never again see Katherine.

Then I hear a mockingbird sing,
I see the dogwoods in bloom,
I look at my barren backyard—
With help from loving friends,
I transform that backyard into a flowering fantasy,
A wonderland of nature's bounty,
A garden dedicated to the memory of Katherine,
Who with her red hair, green eyes, and milky skin,
Had, herself, been one of Nature's kin.

And then one glorious, soul-freeing day,
When I am pruning roses,
Surrounded by Katherine's Garden,
I look and breathe, touch and see, hear and feel.

Life surges all around me.
Life bubbles up through me,
And I am a part of it all,
And Katherine is with me.
I am Demeter and Persephone is with me.
And for the first time in over two years,
I have heartsease.
I am listening intently—
God is speaking to me.

SONDRA: VANITY

During her youth and far beyond,
She and her Vanity were feted;
She and her Vanity were served.
They greedily gorged and feasted on,
The attention and compliments
Her youth and beauty deserved.

Then, too soon, her Vanity demanded
That she repair and restore
Her rapidly wrinkling aging facade.
After winning a hard-fought battle, she
Decided it was time to discard
Her demanding Vanity
And leave unrestored and unrepaired
Her rapidly wrinkling aging facade.

Famished for the flattery and attention
To which it was addicted,
Her Vanity, now confronted
With iron-fisted Reality,
Slowly starved, thrusting her
Into new freedom, released from
The addictive tyranny of Vanity.

KELLY: OUT-MANEUVERED

With an anterior maneuver
       by-passing the perimeter
       of her inhibitions,
Her malicious hormones
       ambushed her good sense,
       lighting a conflagration,
       which consumed
       all sensible restrictions.
Out-gunned by soft brown eyes,
       an elegant nose, auburn hair,
       and a bewitching tail,
She faltered,
       surrendered,
       and took that puppy home.

MILLICENT: DREAMING

Millicent Montgomery, long hair
       gilded silver by invading moonbeams,
Breathing rhythmically in deep REM,
      is dreaming dreams,
Images in flickering technicolor
      darting and shifting,
      shaping and reshaping.

Escaping her curled body,
      wrapped in 500-thread count Egyptian cotton,
      nestled in a king-sized cocoon,
She flashes her VISA to rent a pink cloud.

She drifts above her gated community,
      hovers above the golden domed skyline of Atlanta,
      flits through the mists enveloping the peaks
      of the Appalachian Mountain Range.
Now she is zipping on her green cloud
      through the purple fog over the Atlantic.

Next she is in a room she does not recognize,
      filled with people she does.
A blustering George Bush and a debonaire Tony Blair,
      a grim Madeline Albright and a smiling Jimmy Carter,
      a young Winston Churchill, an older Teddy Roosevelt,
      Benjamin Franklin, between Joseph Stalin and Adolph Hitler,
      Queen Elizabeth, the first, to the left of Julius Caesar,
      Gandhi, Geronimo, Golda Meir, Mao Tse-sung, elbow to elbow,
      And twenty or so more.

Alighting from her silver cloud,
      she is welcomed.

"Just call us by our first names. We are all family here,"
        Benjamin Franklin requests
        as he introduces her, the international expert on peace,
        to her waiting fans.
Graciously, she joins the heads of state and their emissaries,
        taking the seat reserved for her
        at the head of the round table.
"Why don't we vote to stop all wars?
"Why don't we agree to live in peace?" she begins.
"Why don't we agree to devote as much brain power
        and as much scientific study
        to promote peace as
        we do to promote war?"
Then restates her three questions as resolutions.
Whereupon, unanimous, with a show of hands,
        they vote "Yes" to the resolutions.
"Now, let's make a plan," she says,
And that's when the shit hits the fan.
They can't agree on where to start,
        how to proceed,
        and how to end.
Golda stands firm on Palestine, Adolph on Austria.
Joseph and Winston square off at each other,
Madeline glares and Jimmy smiles,
        while the international conference for world peace
        disintergrates into a family brawl.

Retreating, Millicent silently slips away,
        zooming back to reality
        on a mushroom cloud of charcoal gray.

NOEL: PAST

The past is over, he said,
What's done is done,
How you lived before we met is irrelevant,
Our lives started the moment we met,
But I do want to know everything about you,
So tell me,
He cajoled and begged.

A penitent in the confessional,
She poured out names, places, times,
Intimate thoughts and details,
Turning her psyche inside out,
Revealing her heart and soul,
Holding nothing of herself in reserve,
Cooperating in her own robbery.

Surrendering herself, her history,
Destroying any future
They might have had together,
Destroying all chances
Of a shared, continuing story.

RACHEL: FAITH

My church was the center of my universe,
My sole authority on right and wrong,
On what was moral or immoral,
On how to live, what to do, and how.
My faith was inherited and unquestioned
And through it I was made strong.

Then Doubt slithered in, breaching
My unguarded borders,
Whispering, questioning,
Breeding doubts
That bred more doubts
Until one day my faith retreated,
Abandoning me
In cold fogs of non-belief.

Today, weak and naked,
Abandoned, alone,
I wait and wait
Wishing for,
Praying for
The return of my faith.

RUTH: MEMORY

Revisiting the fragile deceptions
Hanging in the Gallery of her Memory,
Fairy tales made of pigment on canvas,
Abstracts more original than
The impressions they usurped.

Refusing to turn a critical gaze
On the images gessoed and painted over,
To disturb the past lurking behind
The illusion of painted beauty,
Accepting the myth of art as truth.

Declining to probe beneath the surface
To the images sealed and painted over,
Celebrating new lines and colors,
Trespassing revisions of revisions
Of truth painted in oils on canvas.

BARBARA: BELIEF

She bartered her present for her future,
Sacrificing today for tomorrow,
Anticipating a transformed life
When her ship would sail into harbor.

Living in the margins of her days,
She spent her youth waiting for tomorrow,
Searching the seas for her treasure ship,
Expecting it to sail into harbor.

She finally spied her ship on the horizon.
Eagerly she watched it sail into harbor.
Inpatient, she opened her treasure chests
And found a shroud, a coffin, and sorrow.

CAMILLA: THE MERRY WIDOW

Matthew, I don't think you ever knew
    just how much I loved you.
Looking forward to every sunrise,
    I believed I was the luckiest woman alive.
Then came the day you came home engulfed
    by the fragrance of her perfume,
    a fragrance revealing her identity,
    a fragrance which shattered my serenity.
I wanted to leave you,
    but there were Janey and Matt,
    who loved you,
    and I had to consider that.
So, I burned my love for your up
    with the intensity of my anger and hurt.
We continued to live together, but apart,
    while vengeance lodged within my heart.
Then your affair ended
    as abruptly as it had begun.

Today, the fifth anniversary of your death,
    is my final visit to your grave.
When two years after you she died,
    died as you did,
    begging for absolution,
    I buried her by your side.
This is now your reality—
    for all eternity
    you two cheaters and betrayers,
    who, guilt-ridden, froze your lust to hate,
    lie together, eternal grave mates.

Now charming gentlemen assist me

with spending your hard earned money,
your insurance and investments,
and all that lovely money she left me.
I have hit the jackpot.
I am healthy and wealthy,
very much alive,
and you and my sister are not.

JANET: THE CHEERLEADER

I was cute,
Big blue eyes, curly blonde ponytail,
Pert nose, outgoing, perky,
A natural athlete,
Perfect cheerleader clay, so—
Not allowed on the playing fields and courts,
I wore the scanty blue and gold uniform,
Screamed and cavorted, exhorted
The Eagles to win, win, win!
Marginalized,
In my place on the sidelines.

I married the former captain of the Eagles,
Produced, supported, and cheered
A daughter, a natural-born athlete,
Who, a generation later,
Excelled on the playing fields and courts.

Today my granddaughter,
Presented with hard-won choices,
Wears the skimpy blue and gold uniform
As she screams and cavorts, exhorting
The Eagles to win, win, win!
In her chosen place—
On the sidelines.

CILLE: SEDUCTION

I planned to clean my house this morning,
To pick things up and tidy them away,
To wash the dishes and mop the floors,
To polish the silver and dust the doors.

But a soft breeze sighed among the trees,
Tickling the rosemary with light fingers,
Tinkling the wind chimes with brief kisses,
Caressing the jasmine climbing the trellis.

A monarch flitted among the daisies,
A spider's web glittered with morning dew,
A mockingbird sang in the gnarled peach tree,
And all outdoors beckoned, beckoned me.

Then dancing on the lawn like a happy child,
Jumping and twisting, enticing, tempting,
A sunbeam called with a seductive smile,
"Come and play with me a little while."

So— what could I do but laugh and follow?
All those plans could wait til the morrow.

CILLE: GARDENIAS

Their fragrance enchants me,
      Luring me from back steps to lily pond,
      Drawing me down the mossy brick path
Bordered by hot pink impatiens, stately hostas,
      And spilling maidenhair ferns.

Their perfume permeates the cool morning air,
      The path turns and there they are—
      Three creamy white blossoms
And four unfurling buds
      Nestled in dew-sparkling glossy green leaves—

Bejeweled perfection—
      Gardenias—
      Ephemeral, elusive, seductive—
Signaling the start of lazy summer days,
      Cooling the air while inflaming the senses—

Prom corsages whispering of secret love,
      Full of promises and first passion
      And the allure of stolen kisses,
Reflecting petal soft faces
      In pastel dresses—

Lazy summer afternoons
      Drifting in front porch swings,
      Dreaming of limitless futures,
The air rich and heavy, casting a spell,
      Cushioned by the scent of gardenia blossoms—

Beguiled into believing that gardenia blossoms,
      Summer and youth—
      Last forever.

CILLE: FIRST PEACH

I stroll past the gnarled peach tree
Reaching for the sun behind the rock wall.
Ripe fruit weighs heavy from its branches.
A scarlet flash, a fluted, "Birdy! Birdy! Birdy!"
And a cardinal lights on an overreaching limb.
The perfume of ripe peaches assaults the air.
Tempting, Tempting—
Reaching out I pluck a golden rose orb,
Weigh its ripe weight in the palm of my hand,
Rub the peach down against my cheek.
The first bite spurts luscious juice,
Which drips from my chin.

CILLE: SUNRISE

Rosalyn, Sweetheart, arise, arise!
Shed Grandma's wedding-ring quilt,
Wash the dreams from you sleepy eyes,
And come see this morning's sunrise.

Come see the wisps of smoky morning mist
         curling above the pond's ripples, whisked
         hither and thither as God exhales,
See the blue heron take wing, circle low, and
         lift off, dusting the steeples of the pines,
See the white eye ring of Mama Wood Duck
         as she ferries chips to her nesting box,
See the quick flash of blue and white
         as you track the kingfisher's flight
         until he is swallowed by the mist,
Watch the doe and her still-spotted fawn
         making a breakfast of crab apple leaves,
         there— on the edge of the south lawn,
Hear the squirrels fussing,
         irritated at our human intrusion,
See the fat rabbit race-hopping for cover,
Listen to the gossiping mockingbirds
         perched atop the muscadine arbor,
Watch the yellow-billed robins fluffing
         their orange and gray feathers
         after the ritual of their daily ablutions,
Now, look to the east, see the rising sun
         once again conquering the horizon.

Rosalyn, Sweetheart, arise, arise!
Come share with me this morning's sunrise.
Dress warmly in blue jeans and red flannel,
Pull on wool socks and worn hiking boots,
Come worship with me in God's Chapel.

100

CILLE: SUMMER STORM

The wind begins as a teasing murmur,
Sighing lightly through the trees,
Accompanied by the gentle hum of soft rain.
Too soon the wind becomes a moan,
Swiftly progressing to a belligerent snarling scream.

Lightning zig-zags across the starless sky,
Briefly illuminating the face of the black night,
Followed, before the count of one,
By cracking, booming thunder.
The rain drums, beating down in penetrating sheets.

Unsecured shutters knock, wanting to come in.
The sharp odor of ozone permeates the cooling air.
Gradually the lightning drifts east,
Followed by the diminishing crescendo of thunder
As the wind dwindles to a whisper.

Raindrops drip softly from eaves and trees
In iambic rhythms against the rock wall.
My room now agleam with slanting moonbeams,
I close my eyes
And slip into peaceful dreams.

CILLE: IF I COULD

If I could fly high and free like a red tailed hawk,
I'd find me one of those thermals and just float,
High up there above the earth,
Just drifting, drifting, drifting—
In lazy circles going round,
Until I catch the movement of a meadow mouse,
Way down there on the ground,
Realize that I skipped lunch,
And dive straight for my supper.

CILLE: SPRINGTIME

When the robin trills her wake-up call,
When jonquils pray by the red barn wall,
When lilies dress-up in Easter white,
And swallowtails waltz in amber light—

It seems I slip the bonds of Earth
And am in step with the universe,
And can dance my way from star to star,
In winged sandals, spangled tights and bra.

Thirty years is not enough time,
Nay, forty, sixty nor ninety-nine,
To experience springtime's annual show,
To see another springtime come and go.

CILLE: MRS. ROBIN RED-BREAST FLIES THE NEST

Mrs. Robin Red-Breast
Was sitting on four eggs about to hatch
In her cozy, but confining, little nest,
When her mate strutted by.

Ruffling the feathers on her breast,
She cooed seductively to him,
  Hey, you, Big Daddy,
  Come on over here and sit on this nest.
  I want to go to town,
  I need to get away,
  I plan to have a ball,
  Now, don't you let me down.

  I don't know what to do,
He whined as he sat down.
  What if the eggs should hatch,
  While you are gone to town?

  Ha, ha,
She laughed with glee
As she flew away and left him sitting there,
  That's what I hope they do, Big Daddy,
  That's what I hope they do.

CILLE: RITUAL

In springtime, early springtime,
The cardinals return.
Scarlet macho males
Sing warning songs to the competitors:
>   Keep away from my territory;
>   Keep away, keep away, or therefore,
>   You'll be the gift the cats leave
>   For the humans at their front door.

Followed by love songs to the fetching females:
>   Purty! Purty! Purty! Birdy! Birdy! Birdy!
>   Hey, Sweet Mama, yes, you, Cool Chick,
>   Wanna build a nest with these nice sticks?
Then like a courting lover,
Bringing chocolates and roses to his sweetheart,
Mr. Cardinal entices the future Mrs. Cardinal
With gifts of seeds garnered from the human's garden cart.

Then they build their nest, absolutely precise,
Raise their fledglings with great self-sacrifice,
And live happily ever after in Red Bird Paradise.

MARGARET: SMOKEYS

They're tearing up another mountain
Each year we come to stay,
  churning the dirt,
  piling it up,
  hauling it away,
Leveling the mountain to build outlet malls
And four-lane highways,
Erasing all traces of the past,
Hauling away the fertile top soil
To build berms at time-share condos,
Berms planted with imported exotics,
Requiring infusions
  of water,
  of phosphates,
Requiring applications
  of herbicides,
  of fungicides,
  of insecticides.
With each rainfall
Cascading down the eroding mountainside
Into icy streams,
Tumbling over the rocks
In spumes of contaminated brown.
We come
  to hike the mountain trails,
  to learn about the native flora,
  to be part of nature's magnitude,
  to enjoy the beauty, the solitude.
We come in our V-8 Dodge Ram
With extended cab,
Stay in our four-room condo
With balcony-view of the mountains.

They're tearing up another mountain
Each time we come to stay,
     churning the dirt,
     piling it up,
     hauling it away.

SHE: SUMMER

Dressed in a flowering shirt,
Sunshine hat and rainbow skirt,
She, a woman of summer bloom,
Golden hair washed in rose perfume,
Roams the plains,
Roams the hills,
Searching for a woman—
A woman of autumn hue,
Russet hair sparkling with evening dew.
Through the last part of June,
All of July and August,
And the first part of September
She searches the plains,
She searches the hills,
Bringing warmth and gentle rains,
Deepening green, ripening grain,
Giving pleasure as she roams.
She finds her woman of autumn hue,
Finds her the third week of September,
Russet hair sparkling with evening dew.
Exhausted, on the edge of sleeping,
She greets the woman of autumn hue
With a yawning breath
And kisses her on the cheek.
Then with her work completed,
She pulls the earth around herself
And settles down to sleep.

SECTION TWO

ELIZABETH: FACES IN THE MIRROR

One day it's my daughter
       I see in the mirror,
The next day it's my mother
       beckoning me.

Caught in the middle,
The present bracketed by reflections
Of time past and time to come,
Adolescence's unlimited promise
       pushing behind,
Middle Age's responsibilities
       holding the center,
Old Age with all its discounts
       leading the line,
Three segments of one matriarchal order
       originating with Eve,
       rooting me in place and time,
       gifting me with a history,
       a present, a future,
Three segments of one continuous line.

VICTORIA: SHOE-SHOE TRAIN

Two-year-old Victoria was playing alone in her room,
Arranging the shoes she had carefully collected,
  From her mama's and papa's closets,
  From under the tables,
  From by the back door,
  From under the beds,
  From under the front porch swing, and
  From the floor in her own little closet.

Her mama's size eights,
Her papa's size tens,
Were placed heel to toe, heel to toe,
  White, black, brown, taupe, and tan,
  Red, pink, navy, purple, and sand,
With her own baby shoes from birth up to twos.
  Oxfords, mary janes, flats, penny loafers, and mules,
  Sandals, high heel pumps, dockers, and running shoes,
Heel to toe, heel to toe,
In a serpentine line snaking across the floor.

When her mama checked in because she was suddenly too quiet,
She looked up and grinned, her eyes full of playful delight.
"Look, Mama, I make shoe-shoe train," she said.
At her mama's look of amazed surprise,
She giggled, "That funny, Mama," the delight still in her eyes.

And then she began to prance and to dance,
Pleased with herself, her mama and papa,
Her first funny joke, and her life in particular.
Then she slipped her plump toddler's feet
Into her mama's red flats,
Scuffling across the floor and singing,

"Look out, Woo-oo-Woo-oo-Woo-oo,
"Look out, Shoe-Shoe Train coming through."

VICTORIA: GIRL CHILD

The summer of her fourth year
She is like a butterfly,
Bewitchingly beguiling,
Unbridled incandescent sunshine,
Twin wings a flutter,
Playing tag among the roses and verbena,
Elusively enchanting,
Ebullient,
Ephemeral.
A flying flower of radial symmetry,
Sapphire and gold,
Laden with happiness,
Rife with promise,
Bursting with life.

MISTY: THAT SMART GIRL

"See that little red-haired girl, Misty,"
I heard my first grade teacher, Mrs. Tandy,
        say to another teacher,
"She's so smart, she scares me.
"I don't know what to do with her."

 I was six years old.
My teacher was fifty.
And I scared her.

Was it because I could read when I was two?
Was it because I could do math in my head?
Was it because I loved languages,
        found them easy to learn?
Was it because she thought
        that I was smarter than she?
Didn't she know she was the adult
        and I the child?

But I was obedient, beautifully behaved,
So, I filled out the work sheets,
Learned to read Mrs. Tandy's way,
Camouflaged,
        so I would fit into her lockstep program,
Stomach aching, scared of her displeasure,
Praying nightly that Mrs. Tandy
        would stop being scared of me,
And that she would somehow
        learn to like me.

JUDY: AUNT NELLIE'S HOME

Hidey places made of quilts and dining room chairs,
Racing down hallways and creeping up stairs,
Daring to catch Aunt Nellie unawares—

I loved to go to Aunt Nellie's home,
Plump Aunt Nellie, with a husband long dead
And two children grown, three dogs and two cats,
An untidy kitchen smelling of fresh baking bread,
Date scones piled high on a blue willow plate,
A jug of cream and a pot of orange marmalade,
Served with milk spiked with a drop of tea
With a gray tabby purring on my scabby knee.

Playing dress-up in Aunt Nellie's old hat,
Swooping to nibble her irresistible wrinkled neck
In my role of wicked, blood-thirsty Vampire Bat—

Providing sanctuary to a child starved for fantasy,
Aunt Nellie understood the charm of imperfection,
The allure of the slightly off-center,
The welcome of identifying, defining clutter.
For my mother pristine was a prime requirement,
Perfection her holy grail,
She decorated her house in beige monochrome,
But Aunt Nellie loved her house into a home.

Zooming around Aunt Nellie's bedroom
On a hobby horse make from the handle of a broom,
Never-minding the antiques and heirlooms.

CINDY: TWELFTH SUMMER

"Mommy, my dolls won't talk to me any more,"
She sobbed.
And thus in her twelfth summer, robbed
Suddenly of the long-running dialogues
She had held with her dolls since she could remember,
She packed them in two storage cartons
In green tissue paper with rose-scented sachets,
And with a purple marker
Labeled them Cindy's Dolls,
Listing their names in alphabetical order,
Tied the cartons with silver and gold ribbons,
Intertwined with sprigs of dried lavender,
And lovingly banished them from their home
In her light-filled pink and yellow room
Into a barren attic corner.

The next day she purchased,
With money she had saved for an American Girl doll,
Ruby and sapphire paint for the walls of her room,
A size thirty double A bra,
Iridescent eye shadow,
And a shocking poster of an adolescent rock star.

JILL: YOUNG LOVE

if I start to like a BOY a lot
I lose my cool composure when HE's around
my palms get disgustingly sweaty
my tongue feels thick and bound
and the beat of my heart goes thump-er-tee-bop-dot
and I worry if HE likes ME or not

but if a BOY starts to like ME a lot
my cool composure comes roaring back
HIS palms get disgustingly sweaty
HIS tongue seems to run off track
and the beat of HIS heart goes thump-er-tee-bop-dot
and HE's worried if I like HIM or not

sometimes I think just being friends is best
without the aggravation and the stress
of wondering if HE likes ME as much as I like HIM
but—I'd miss the drama of starring in MY own poem

TARA: SIXTEEN

When I see old women rocking on front porches,
Shod in velcro-fastened black oxfords,
Defenseless against Time and Gravity,

When I see old women sitting on front porches,
Dressed in elastic-waisted pastel knits,
Lovers long ago buried and forgiven,

When I see old women watching, without envy,
Laughing young lovers as they pass,
Passion a long forgotten inconvenience,

When I see old women gossiping, while
Dodging Death, on front porches,
I see a flash of my future,

And I gamble that I won't live forever,
And I wager that,
Cheating Time and Gravity, I die young

From a surfeit of loving and hating,
From excessive excitement and danger,
And that I depart this world

In a thundering blaze of glory,
Eulogized and elegized,
At the apex of my life's story.

CATHY: SHOULD I?

Should I get married?
Should I be good?
Should I follow my mother's footsteps
The way she says I should?
Should I be a good wife and mother, no surprises,
But get a good education so I can support my family
If some day the need arises?

Should I get married?
Should I be good?
Should I restrict myself to one partner,
Live in a suburban neighborhood?
Should I produce two children, no third, no fourth,
Replacing just my husband and me
For zero population growth?

Should I get married?
Should I be good?
Should I live my life for me,
Or live my life the way she says I should?
Should I move seamlessly from girlhood to womanhood,
And like her, live for others,
Forgetting myself and losing my personhood?

Should I get married?
Should I be good?
The safe answer is probably yes,
But the answer to will I—
That's anybody's guess.

MOLLY: THE BEQUEST

My soul absorbed the singing words
That lifted me beyond my world
Of single Mom and absent Dad,
Of frequent moves and poverty.

Each precious word enriched my soul,
Which grew robust in fertile soil,
Enabling me to conquer fear
And breach the walls of my prison.

This gift of wealth—a library card—
Bequeathed to me a world of books,
Which freed my soul and planted hope
And gave me strength so I could thrive.

SUELLEN: READJUSTING THE MIRRORS

in the garden of my mind
with all the fire centered in my heart
knowing from birth I was not like others
saying one thing while thinking another
telling a story no one heard

courting conformity to save my head
        [afraid to let my head rise above the crowd]
camouflaged
trying my damnedest to blend
to fit in
to break the iron shackles of one-of-a-kind uniqueness
        [afraid my head would be sliced off
            whish! whish! just like that]
negating self to be allowed to join the game

readjusting the mirrors
looking behind me at reflections
of multiples of me avoiding my eyes—
at multiples of me diminishing in size—

LORI: ALISON

Alison— Curly blonde hair,
Long slim legs, flawless skin,
Warm, charming, A-plus average,
Homecoming queen perfection—
The Senior Helen of Hilton High.
I worshiped Alison as only an awkward Freshman could—
From afar.

One afternoon I sat writing in the school library,
Oblivious of students surrounding me.
Intruding into my solitude,
Gracing me with her Crest-perfect smile, Alison asked,
        May I join you?
        I want to talk to you a little while.
At my dumb nod,
She slid her stack of books onto the table and pulled up a chair.
        I've been wanting to talk to you,
She confided.
At my second dumb nod, she continued,
        I've been noticing you around school,
        And I wanted to tell you how much you remind me
        Of myself three years ago.
She had my full attention,
Even though my tongue was glued tight in my mouth.
        Like you, I was always pretty,
        And like you, smart, too,
        Just a victim of my heredity and environment,
She laughed and patted her psychology textbook.
        I noticed you writing.
        I want to invite you to work on the school newspaper.
        I have an application right here,
        And I'll help you fill it out now.

She sat and talked with me for an hour
And then drove me home.
I walked up the steps to my house,
Smiling, shoulders straight,

Facing my reflection in the glass of the front door—
Short, rounded figure, curly black hair,
Brown eyes, milk chocolate skin—
      Just another product of your heredity and environment,
I heard her whisper.
      But you become what you make of it.

A thought haunts me still—
How could she have known of the suicide note
I concealed in my English notebook as she sat down,
And the razor I planned to use when I reached home?

LAURA: THAT WAS THEN

She was barely seventeen,
An honor student,
Brilliant, charming, beautiful,
Pregnant.

Knowing that I was Pro-Choice,
She asked me to lend her money
For a termination.
She never used the A word.

I gave her cash,
She gave me her IOU,
Although I assured her the money
Was a gift, not a loan.

I volunteered to go with her.
She said, "No, thank you."
It was her problem
And she would deal with it alone.

She refused to involve
Her teenage partner
And vowed she'd die
Before telling her parents.

She graduated, didn't keep in touch.
Years later I received cash in an envelope,
No return address, no cancellation mark,
No note.

I saw her on the news last night,
Protesting outside a Family Planning Clinic,
Part of a group
From the Far Right.

FREDA: ESCAPE

After breaking through the iron barriers,
When freedom and liberty are finally mine,
The dream a reality of endless singing,
I travel toward the eastern sun,
Following the beckoning road as it unwinds,
With one eye looking back over my shoulder
At what I'm leaving behind,
The other eye looking to the splendors awaiting—
Following the twisting road as it unwinds.

JANE: SUMMER LOVE

She'll never forget those
    enchanted summer nights,
When beguiled by the fragrance
    of roses and turquoise skies,
They dined and danced in
    Summer's seductive lights,
And she saw love reflected
    in the blue of his eyes.

Of course, she felt it and meant it
    when she would declare,
She'd love him forever and ever
    plus one extra day,
Yet two years later when she met
    him in the town square,
She introduced James Jones
    to her new love as John Jay.

AMBER: IF SHE COULD GO ON OPRAH

Her overriding ambition is to appear on OPRAH,
But she has no idea how—
She was not abused as a child or as a wife
Nor is she an abuser,
She doesn't suffer from depression
Nor does anyone in her family,
Nor are they or she addicted to
Drugs, alcohol, work, sex, or chocolate
(well, maybe to TV),
She has not overcome dyslexia
Or attention deficit syndrome
Nor any other syndrome,
Nor has she recently lost two hundred pounds.
She can't write or sing or act,
She can't even tell a joke,
Has made no discoveries,
Has not heroically saved the life of her worst enemy,
Nor invented a better mouse trap.
She is common,
Ordinary,
Average,
Run-of-the-mill—
Nevertheless, if she could just be on OPRAH,
She'd set her VCR to tape her appearance,
So she could see herself on TV again and again.
For the rest of her life she would be somebody,
She would have arrived (where she wasn't sure),
She would have proof of her importance—
And of her existence.

RITA: THE GOOD TIME GIRL

Dressed in gaudy party clothes,
We burned our candles
Both day and night.

Our fires—
Dancing, prancing,
Twirling, whirling,
Advancing, retreating,
Partying without ceasing.

Loosening our spirits,
Finding our bliss
In crystal sparks of delight,
Hearts blazing
In blue and crimson,
Dancing day and night.

Our candles burning
Intense, fast, bright—
Banishing ghosts
In hot white.

Flames racing
Toward the center,
Colliding,
Consuming each other—
Flickering—Dying—
Extinguished.

PAULA: LOSING TO WIN

Like a racehorse bred for competition,
      she has been conditioned to excel
      by her parents and their hired coaches.

Showing opponents no mercy,
      never walking away from a dare,
      always embracing a challenge—

Driven to collect blue ribbons and gold medals,
      anything less than first unthinkable,
      coming close only counting in horseshoes—

Feeling alive—that she exists
      when she is striving, competing—
      running a race—

Knowing she's only as good as her next promotion,
      her next gold medal,
      or her next first place.

JENNIFER: DYING TO BE THIN

She always heard,
And she believed every word,
            You can't be too rich or too thin.
Believing that rich would come after thin,
She tried every diet, sensible or absurd,
Religiously counting calories, weighing grams,
Keeping a diary of every bite of food eaten.

The cushioning, softening layers of fat dissolved,
Melting, dripping away—
Leaving skin, leaving bones.
She was winning, winning—
For once in her life in total control.
She was becoming beautiful, elegant,
            fashionable, desirable—
Looking great in her size 4 jeans.

As she became slim, slimmer—
            thin and even thinner,
Her breasts, emptied of fat,
            flapped like puppy dog ears,
Her once round cheeks caved in,
Her concave stomach framed by jutting pelvic bones,
Her butt flat as two stones.
With pencil straight thighs,
            she could cross her stockinged legs,
With never a whispering sigh to suggest soft flesh.
She was beautiful, elegant, fashionable, desirable—
Looking fantastic in her size 0 jeans.

She became so thin the world could hardly see her.
She became so thin, that like Karen Carpenter,
One day she just faded away—
            and ceased to be.

JAMIE: CHOICES

It's clear as hindsight to me
Your mind and mine will never agree.
You love the hives of your city,
The crowds, the noise, the energy.
Give me a cottage and a garden,
Good books, a cat, friends visiting often.

The quiet life for me,
The frantic for you,
Your life would tire me,
And mine would bore you,
Yet you love me
And I love you.

What's that you say?
Let's choose the day?
Well, then, Lover,
I choose Sunday.

VIOLET: BIOLOGICAL CLOCK

When I was one and twenty, I said to you:
When a yellow rose blooms in three feet of snow,
When a snowball doesn't melt in hell,
When gold and silver on apple trees grow,
When cows can bark and dogs can moo,
  Then I might fall in love with you.

When I was six and twenty, I said to you:
When a pecan shell grows into a magnolia tree,
When a colony of humans settle on the sun,
When the sun rises in the north and then floats free,
When rain falls up and lies are true,
  Then I might even marry you.

When I was one and thirty, I said to you:
Who cares that snowballs melt in hell,
Who cares where the sun rises and sets,
Who cares that on the sun no humans dwell,
That cows can't bark and dogs can't moo,
  Just ask me again and I'll marry you.

DANICE: TROPHY WIFE

Desiring me with cold passion,
His thirst to accumulate the best
            unquenchable,
He strategically plotted his quest,
Utilizing the same measures used
            in acquiring his treasures.

Outbidding other potential buyers,
He bought me,
Procuring me
            by paying more than
The asking price
            for trophy wives.

Thus, I froze my beauty and youth
In the ice of his old man's bed
            of power and wealth,
And even though generations
            and social classes divided us,
I filled my niche with panache.

Refining his collections,
Trading up for new acquisitions,
He sold lesser
            to purchase better,
Relentless in his quest
            to possess the best.

In time,
Tagged with impeccable provenance,
I was auctioned at fair market value
And replaced by a new trophy wife,

Whose quality and asking price
were higher than mine.

THERESA: PAID IN FULL

She was the only child of parents
Who daily itemized each sacrifice
They made for her
And presented her with
The detailed bill of payment
They expected in return.

Hobbled by love and guilt
And a carefully cultivated
Sense of filial duty, foregoing
All personal preferences,
She paid the bill in full
Just as it was presented.

They never asked—
Nor did she ever say—
How she felt about paying
For her life their way.

LYNN: CHANGING

Through infatuated eyes
She saw him as malleable male clay
Waiting for her shaping and molding.

He had the emotional range of middle C,
The emotional capacity of algae.

But—

She would wake him up,
Connect him to his feelings,
Warm him up,
She just needed to adjust his emotional thermostat
To change him— (snap!) just like that!

Five years later
Inside the dust smeared windows of their marriage
The weak winter sunlight tries to wedge a way in
While he retains the emotional range of middle C,
The emotional response of algae.
And she—
She is his wife, his maid, his mother—
Daydreaming of twenty ways to
        commit the perfect murder.

BETTY SUE: HUNTING SEASON

Tall, young, rich, and handsome preferred—
But, she'll take what she can find—
Short or tall,
Blonde, brunette, auburn— or no hair at all,
Blue eyes, brown eyes, gray or green,
Young, old, or in between,
Athlete or studious nerd,
Country, gown, or town,
It matters not at all
As long as he's an eligible male
And responds to her mating call.
Her rifle is loaded for husband
And pointed straight at her prey,
Unless he's a master of evasive tactics,
He'll soon find himself promising
      To love, honor, and obey.

IRIS: RED DUST

Her lover in the grip of lust,
Swears his devotion in red dust,
Stamps his word on a rushing river,
Writes his love on a moonbeam sliver,
Plights his troth in a spider's web,
Vows fidelity on the ocean's ebb.
To win her, he swears what he must;
'Tis a shame he swears in red dust.

'Tis a shame and a pity
His love is so lightly spoken;
His troth is so often broken.
'Tis a shame and a pity
If once again his troth he plights,
She'll be back in his arms tonight.

TINA: MAKE ME A DEITY

It was as if God said to me:
>Don't change your life
>on my account;
>I'm just passing through.
He took His hat.
He won't be coming back.

Damn!
His leaving left a void.

I desire to be intimately
connected to a Divine,
to a Universal Mother
who is roundly curved
and whose hat always
hangs in my home.
I need a nurturing goddess,
a deity cast in a female mold.
Yes! I want a Matriarch
forged for my woman's soul.

RONI: BLANK PAGE

Seeking the golden hand
　　　to write on the blank page
　　　filling it with words—

Scribbling
　　　in red, in green
　　　in blue, in black—

Explaining life
　　　defining infinity, eternity
　　　breaching reality—

Searching for the golden hand
　　　to fill in the blank space
　　　to cover the empty page—

With words, enough words
　　　perhaps she will comprehend
　　　perhaps she will understand.

HAYLEY: THE WILD YEARS

Those were the wild years, the free years,
When untamed, unrestrained,
I indulged in marathon shopping sprees,
Maxing credit cards past their limits,
My adoring father paying the bills.
Larking about, seeking new thrills,
Daring the gods, risking the odds,
Gambling my life, my freedom,
Living an idyll of time standing still.

My youth and beauty potent,
I was stalked by hunters of Sex,
Trappers of Wives
Baiting velvet traps with promising lies.
And too soon I became a willing captive,
Caged, domesticated, passive,
Partner in my own metamorphosis
Into submissive tame prey
Found in any supermarket.

Where did they go,
Those wild years, those free years?
How did I become a prisoner
In my own life?

JEAN: MARRIAGE

You and I forged Us and We
merging Our discrete identities
mutual concessions
a compromise of unity
sharing heart sharing soul
I crossing the threshold into Your world
You crossing the threshold into Mine
making Our separate worlds one whole
giving-taking in equal parts
I your heart and bliss
You My soul and passion
negotiating harmony
indivisible
YouMe
together
Us and We

JEAN: DIVORCE

You and I lost Our Us and We
in tongues of profound silence
doors locked against the whole
You in a world as small as a heart
I in a world as big as a soul
keys lost that unlock a mutual threshold
forgetting how to mingle
the soul of I and the heart of You
You with the bliss of Your solitude
I with the passion of My obsession
separate
apart
divisible
You—Me
no longer Us
no longer We

CAROL: WIDOW

In the dead ebony of night
Abruptly awaking to my mortality,
Obsessed by the if-only of grief,
Alternating with waves of anger
At what was beautiful
    And is no more.

Bereft,
I reach for him,
Once my comfort, my safeguard
Against the promenading demons
Of the dark, He—
    Now one of them—

Lured from my bed
By irresistible Death—
And I the deserted, the betrayed,
Alone—waking to reality,
Craving the oblivion of sleep—
    Dreamless, endless sleep.

CAROL: ONE OF ONE

Catapulted from the marriage bed
      Of one of two
      To a single one of one,
Widowed too young, but
      Feeling too old to go on living,
Fighting my way through the stages of grieving,
Achieving a compromising acceptance as
      Loving memories of the past
      Replaced if-only and raging anger.

Finally realizing I liked—
      Finding my book where I had left it,
      The thermostat in my control,
      Scissors and hammer in their places,
      Car seat and mirrors adjusted,
      Radio permanently tuned to NPR,
      Having a whole bed,
      No covers snatched,
      No sleep interrupted by snoring
      And jabs from elbows and knees,
      Dining when hungry,
      Eating what I please—

Somewhere beyond
      The shrouding mist of memory,
      There are now fleeting hopes
      Of becoming one of two again.
Like a kaleidoscope,
      The design of my life kept changing,
      Year by year,
      Until contented aloneness
      Replaced grieving loneliness.

CAROL: TWO BY TWO

After I had given up hope
Of being one of two again,
I met Joe—
 Younger than I,
 Shorter, too,
 Earning less money—
 The three no-nos of my youth—
But, oh, how he reminded me
 Of the pleasures
 Of living life two by two.

Widowed with two children, he
 Offered a life lived four by four.
One by one the old prejudices melted,
 Dissolving in encompassing love.
It has taken compromise,
 More giving than taking,
It has taken time
 Learning to live in harmony
 With this younger lover of mine.

Like a kaleidoscope,
 The design of my life kept changing—
Until I became one of two again—
 And one of four for the first time.

GAIL: REMARRIAGE

Before your family and mine intertwine,
Before we make plural our separate single,
Before your two and my three mingle,
Fused by our matrimony—

We should consider
That you failed twice
And I failed trice
To achieve lasting wedded bliss.

You think that this,
The third time for you,
The fourth for me,
Can't miss.

Good grief—
I'm marrying an optimist.

ELLEN: THE MONDAY AFTER LABOR DAY

The Yellow Dragon shrieks
To a halt,
Its left wing flapping,
Gobbles her three sons,
Then snorting and belching,
Vanishes
With her three treasures,
Hostages
In its Yellow Dragon belly.

She stands by the mailbox,
Hands lifted in silent supplication,
Sacrificing her peace of mind
For their safe return.
She spends her day
Planning, preparing,
Waiting for
The Yellow Dragon's return,
Waiting for her life to begin again
When the Yellow Dragon
Releases her three sons.

MICHELE: THE MONDAY AFTER LABOR DAY, SECOND VERSION

I'm tap dancing on the counter tops,
Doing ballet in the dining room,
And waltzing with my mops.

I'm turning cart wheels down the hall,
Back flips in the living room,
And doing head stands against the wall.

I'm somersaulting down the stairs,
Leaping over the couch,
And hopscotching from tables to chairs.

I'm happily slapping my knee,
And I'm grinning from ear to ear
When I'm not chuckling with glee.

It's the Monday after Labor Day,
Yes! My three Musketeers—
Went back to school today.

RUSSELL: THAT MEAN GIRL

They said,
>She's the meanest girl in the county.

And They said,
>A mean girl is ten times worse than a mean boy.

I heard Them, but, I thought I was just me,
And, if being me meant being mean,
Then, by golly, I was mean.
Maybe it was because I was quick to take offense,
And used my fists in effective defense. Anyway—
I wore my pants, played my ball,
Swam naked in Coldwater Creek,
Hunted and fished with the boys,
Outran them all. And, thus—
I grew strong and tall.

I went to Auburn University,
Became an engineer.
When I was pushing thirty,
Working a project in Tennessee,
I met a fellow engineer.
He introduced me to his parents:
>This is the meanest woman in the county,
>And I plan to marry her.

What can I say?
I loved that man, so I married him,
And we started our own engineering firm.

In time we had two daughters.
My husband hopes They say,
And I agree with him,
About our daughters, too,
>They're the meanest girls in the county,
>They take after their Mama— those two.

151

DONNA: OUT OF CONTROL

Like a dragon hoarding his silver and gold,
My husband protected me with a steel stranglehold—
  for my own good,
Guarding, manipulating, isolating—
  for my own good,
Imprisoning, controlling—
  for my own good—

I believed him, blaming myself,
When he shouted at me, out of control—
  Clean this stinking house!
  What do you do all day?
  I can't eat this slop!
  Why can't you cook Mama's way?
  You lazy bitch!
  Why can't you control those kids?
  That's woman's work— your job.
  Why can't you fix your hair, lose weight?
  You're such a slob.
  No one else could stand to have sex with you.
  NO! Your friends can't come over.
  I'm watching the ball game on TV.
  NO! You can't visit your mother.
  Your job is to take care of me.
  No one else could love or understand you,
  No one else would tolerate the stupid things you do,
  It's all your fault that I have to hit you.
  Don't ever think about leaving me— Never.
  Don't you understand that I love you?
  You are mine and will be mine forever.

DONNA: THE GIFT

Fleeing in the dead of night,
Escaping that dark abode,
Freeing ourselves from the dragon's control,
Fleeing from love gone sour,
  from too much hurt and hate,
  from too much withholding of self.

Empty-handed—thingless,
Forsaking hindering burdens from our past,
Just my two girls and me, just we three,
Each step lighter than the last,
Stumbling upon your beckoning light,
Sending golden fingers out to welcome me
  and my two girls, all three.

You gave us sanctuary,
Safety at the end of our flight,
But the richest gift of all you gave us—
You gave us healing light.

MILLIE: APRON STRINGS

I helped my love to go away,
I helped him pack his gear.
After checking his closet
And under his bed,
We carried the boxes to his car
And stowed them neatly in the rear.

I hugged and kissed him one last time
And gave him last-minute advice,
Then waved him on his way.
At the end of the drive,
He stopped his car.
The phone in my hand beeped twice.

"See, Mom," he laughed at me,
"At Georgia Tech I'll be okay —
"Just two phone rings away."
He tapped his horn,
Beep, beep,
Then waved and sped away.

ELLEN: EMPTY NEST

The brick house echoes
With the sounds of
       Slamming doors,
       Pounding footsteps,
       Shouted greetings,
       Booming laughter,
       The bounce of basketballs,
       The thunk of baseballs.
"Mom, what's for dinner?"

With lingering smells of
       Spilt chocolate milk,
       Hamburgers and french fries,
       Pepperoni and cheese pizza,
       Sweaty boys,
       Gym shoes and socks,
       Chamomile lotions and Ace bandages.
"Mom, where are my gym shorts?"

With after images of
       Books thrown in the hall,
       A driveway filled with bikes,
       Ping pong in the garage,
       Scraped knees,
       Skates on the stairs,
       Frisbees floating through the air.
"Mom, where are the band-aids?"

With ghosts of three boyhoods outgrown,
Images of three grown men superimposed,
Pregnant with unasked questions—
       Are you eating your vegetables?

Do you floss every day?
Must you live so far away?
Do you have enough money?
Do you need a loan?
Are you happy?
When are you coming home?

MICHELE: EMPTY NEST, SECOND VERSION

I'm doing laundry once a week
     while listening to classical jazz,
Parking the car in the middle of the carport,
     ripping out the basketball court,
Planting roses and perennial borders,
     decorating new guest quarters,
Controlling the cable remote
     while watching TV in my housecoat,
Not cooking much,
     meeting friends for cocktails and lunch,
Reading the newspaper from front to back
     with the sports pages intact,
Taking line dancing classes,
     Substituting contacts for eyeglasses,
Renewing my passport
     and buying milk by the quart.

No more PTA, no more candy sales,
     no more coordinating schedules,
No more waiting up late,
     sleeping until I wake,
Having the couch,
     heck, the whole house,
All to myself

Since the last of my three Musketeers
     started college in September
And the oldest Musketeer took the dog
     to his new home in December.

ESTHER: RECOVERY

After the diagnosis—
During the treatment—
Working hard to beat the odds
  of her fifty-fifty chance of recovery.

Inspired with gifts from the gardens
  of her friends,
With firm expectations of seeing
  the results of her labor,
She plants bulbs and roots,
  sows seeds,
  propagates cuttings and shoots.
Given in friendship, nourished with love,
They flourish.

Grateful to see the miracles brought
  by each new day,
Finding in Nature's open-handed palm
  soothing calm,
  healing balm,
Waking to see the results of her labor,
Day by day she tips the percentages
  in her favor.

IDELLA: THE PIANO PLAYER

She leaves the beds unmade,
Lets the dishes drain,
Plays the piano and sings
Country, jazz, classic, swing—

She leaves the floors unswept,
Lets the dinner burn,
Plays the piano and sings
Gospel, blues, ragtime, pop—

She leaves the clothes unironed,
Lets the water run,
Plays the piano and sings
New age, soul, opera, rock.

But— her husband and children
Just want to be fed,
Always have clean clothes,
And fresh linen on their beds.

MARYANN: IT USED TO BE

It used to be that he and I
    would lie in bed talking,
    sometimes half the night,
Facing each other,
Reliving our day,
Planning our future,
Sharing feelings, thoughts, love,
Feeding our marriage with
    a bounty of nourishing words.

Now he reads his magazine.
I read my mystery.
He pecks me on the cheek
    as he switches off his lamp,
    turns his back and sleeps.
I close my book,
    carefully marking my place
    as if it matters,
    switch off my lamp
    and begin counting the hours
    in time to his rhythmic snoring.

Wondering why he stopped his kisses,
Wondering why he hoards his words,
Starved for the nourishment
    of our lost talking.

MARYANN: STOLEN KISSES

with whispered words and soft caresses
Tony wakes me with his kisses
along my cheeks
across my brow

I reach out to return his kisses
he evades my embrace
dodges my kisses

now that I am fully awake
no more kisses along my cheeks
across my brow
no more Tony stealing kisses
no more Tony any how

if I can go back to sleep
(despite my husband's rumbling snoring)
maybe Tony will again creep
out of my subconscious

to steal more kisses from my lips
bestow more kisses along my cheeks

MITZI: THE ENEMY

Fighting Time's impartiality,
His unfair fairness,
His inexorable linear advances—

Sparing no expense,
Employing every artifice
At her disposal—
The major weapons
Of conquest and defense
Stockpiled in her arsenal
Impotent when deployed
Against advancing Time.

Meanwhile Time never falters,
Never flinches
At the barricades and trenches
Of her Maginot Line.
She retreats, retrenches,
But Time keeps marching,
Conquering youth,
Plundering beauty
Birthday by birthday,
Attacking, breaching
All her fortified defenses.

MITZI: INVISIBLE

At 5 p.m. Friday the revolving door thrust her
Into the din and heat of Cadbury Square,
Sunglasses fogging.
Four workers in yellow hard hats
Restoring the facade of the Bonner Bank Building,
Whistled and yelled,
        Hey, hey, Foxy Mama, it's Friday.
        Wanna get down and party dirty?
Then the youngest grabbed his crotch on a dare
And danced a suggestive jig in Cadbury Square.

At 5 p.m. Monday the revolving door thrust her
Into the din and heat of Cadbury Square,
Sunglasses fogging.
Restoring the facade of the Bonner Bank Building,
Four workers in yellow hard hats
Did not see her,
Could not see her
Since she had crossed the Age Divide
Into invisibility on Saturday.
After the celebration of her first
Woman-of-a-Certain-Age birthday,
Not one construction worker
Whistled or yelled at her,
Grabbed his crotch on a dare,
Or danced a suggestive jig in Cadbury Square.

YONNE: MATRIARCH

You are like the lion cubs,
The pampered princesses
And princes of the savannah,
Dancing from then to now and to after.
The wind cooling your heat,
The sun heating your cold,
The dew and the rain quenching your thirst,
Curious, hard playing,
Swatting a bee, tasting its sting,
Purring as you dream,
A soft, sleepy, trusting rumble,
The grass your feather bed,
The clouds your coverlet,
The moon singing a lullaby,
Backed by the humming stars,
As you slumber, safe, secure.

I am like the wise lioness,
The matriarch of the savannah,
Lying in the sun,
Watching in the rain,
Guarding in the night,
Protecting and guiding,
Loving you with every heartbeat.
Bittersweet,
Watching you growing up at my feet.

YONNE: JUST READING

I planned to do the shopping today,
To buy the groceries and put them away,
To cash a check and pick up the cleaning,
To purchase the gifts that give Christmas meaning.

But sliding around on the seat by my knee
Were twelve overdue books that were going to cost me
An arm and a leg and my good citizenship star
If I didn't return them before driving too far.

First on my orderly route designed to save time
Came the public library located on Vine.
I returned the twelve books; paid a ten dollar fine,
Allowed ten minutes for new acquisitions, so divine.

F—Charles Frazier, I still haven't read COLD MOUNTAIN,
    Everyone keeps telling me that the story is genuine.
H—MISERY LOVES MAGGODY, by mystery writer, Joan
Hess,
    Will Arly get Ruby Bee and Estell out of their latest mess?
H—Tony Hillerman's THE FIRST EAGLE, featuring Leaphorn
and Chee,
    The Navaho tribal policemen, entices me.
M—Frank McCourt's 'TIS, the sequel to ANGELA'S ASHES,
    I'll take it too; now, where are my glasses?

I found a small table and chair in the corner,
Planning to read just half an hour, no longer.
COLD MOUNTAIN I finished; loved every word.
MISERY LOVES MAGGODY, delightfully absurd.

Then Hillerman's Joe Leaphorn and Jim Chee

Creatively solved another Navaho mystery.
I was starting on 'TIS when I felt a tap on my arm,
"We're closing now." I blinked in alarm.

Then the world returned with a crash and a clang,
And up from the armchair I hastily sprang,
A glance at my watch told me it was six in the evening.

I had spent the whole day just reading and reading.

Now, there are those who say my day was ill-spent,
That the reading of books never helped pay the rent.
I do not think that I wasted my day,
Was it ill-spent? Reader, what do you say?

YONNE: I'VE GOT YOUR NOSE

At the age of two or so,
She was playing with her Poppy,
When he gently took her nose,
Between his index and middle finger,
And pulling his hand away,
Inserted his thumb between the two, and said
      I've got your nose.
Bouncing in her pink tennis shoes, she begged,
      Let me see; let me see!
      Poppy, let me see!
Her Poppy laughed, and, going to the backdoor,
Pretended to throw her nose away.
Tears began to stream from her moss green eyes,
As she begged her Poppy,
      Put it back; put it back;
      Go get it, Poppy.
      I want my nose put right back.
Faster than the speed of light,
SuperPoppy raced into the back yard,
Pretended to find her nose,
Raced back in and replaced the nose
On her upturned face.
      There, your nose is where it should be.
      I'm sorry, Sweetheart,
He reassured her, wiping her tears.
      That's O.K., Poppy.
      But you should think before you act,
She admonished him.
      I'll have to put you in time out, so
      You'll think before you act next time.
Sticking the wayward nose into the air,
Tossing her head, and saying,

Umph!

She permitted her Poppy to leave her Royal Presence.

YONNE: PRECEDENCE

I planned to write five pages today,
Revise two chapters and file them away,
Research the history and fine tune the plot,
Recheck the time line; get an early start.

But— as I switched on the computer,
The telephone started to ring.
  Hello,
I absent mindedly muttered,
My preoccupied brain busy composing.
  Gran,
My five-year-old granddaughter said,
Her voice soft and clear.
    I have a slight fever. I have to stay in bed.
    Mom won't let me go to school.
    Would you read me a story?
    One that would make me feel all nice and cool.
I asked,
    Over the phone or in person?
She sighed,
    The phone if you can't come;
    But in person is best.
I switched off the computer,
Locked it down tight,
And picked up a stack of books,
A sick child's delight,
About giants and dragons in far away places,
And the Grinch who stole Christmas
On Christmas Eve Night.

In the grand scheme of life,
I wish to make clear,

A sick granddaughter who wants to hear,
Stories about dinosaurs, fairies, princesses and such,
Outranks five pages, two chapters, and historical research.

YVONNE: WHAT MEANS ACCEPT?

"Gran?"
"Yes, Sweetie?"
"What means accept?"

Absolute means absolute,
And hat means hat,
And there are many words in English like that,
That say exactly what they mean,
And mean exactly what they say,
And don't confuse young children in any way.

But there are words such as accept,
Which can mean embrace, take up, welcome, receive,
Admit, take in, approve, endure, assent, or believe,
Where the meaning all depends,
On how it is said and where and when,
And on the speaker's and listener's intellectual acumen.

"Gran?"
"Yes, Sweetie?"
"What means acumen?"

YONNE: THE TWENTY-ONE-MONTH-OLD HOUDINI

My daughter called me on Wednesday.
I had to give Little Man a spanking today,
She said when I answered the telephone.
Why? I asked, surprised and dismayed at her tone.

I was driving down Riverside Drive,
With your grandson in the back seat,
Strapped securely into his child-proof car seat.
When I heard him giggle, I knew what it meant.
He had climbed, yet again, out of that child-proof seat.
While I looked for a safe spot to pull off the busy street,
He climbed from the back and into the front seat
And tried to open the locked passenger door.
I swung into Riverside Used Car Lot,
Just in time to prevent him from opening the door,
And falling out on his stubborn blonde head.
I unbuckled my seat belt, ran around to his side,
And there in that used car lot I tanned his little hide.
He cried and he yelled
While three salesmen watched in disapproval
With cell phones in hand, ready to call DFACS.
But I hugged him and kissed him,
And tried to explain:
That while the car was in motion, he must stay strapped in,
That I loved him and loved him and loved him again.
He let me wipe the tears from his rosy cheeks,
Then he looked at me with his luminous blue eyes,
Threw his little boy arms around my neck,
And hiccupped, I sorry, Mommy. Love Mommy.
And I melted inside.
I then marched up and faced three disapproving frowns
And explained about my little Houdini.

As one, they said, Give him three more spankings,
One for each of us, and we all laughed in relief.

If I raise this ladder-climbing, playpen-escaping boy child,
To be an adult full grown,
He'll charm all the girls and their Mamas and Papas.
But, by then every hair on my head,
Will be whiter than gray.
Lord, give me the wisdom to know when to catch him,
The wisdom to know when to leave him alone.
And the wisdom to know when to push him on his way,
I pray every day.

Four days later on an overcast December morning,
I picked up the telephone.
Hello, I said.
Mama, it's me, my daughter replied.
What's he done this time? I asked with dread.
Oh, she laughed. Nothing too bad.
Just a couple of bumps to the head.
I'm sitting here on the edge of the front porch
Watching Her Ladyship pick red berries off the dogwood tree,
While Little Man—
Just then I heard,
Mommy, I jum-pp! Mommy, I jum-pp!
What's he doing? I interrupted.
Jumping off the bottom step with both feet at the same time.
How's he doing? I asked.
Falling occasionally, but getting right up and jumping again.
Just look at that. Now, he's jumping from the second step.
Just listen:
Came the exultant little boy voice over the telephone,
Mommy, I jum-pp! Mommy, I jum-pp!

YONNE: E-MAIL

She e-mails news of
Watching sparrows and tufted tit-mice
Jockeying at the bird feeder
Outside the kitchen window,
Of her son's climbing the stairs by himself
And her daughter's request
To have the training wheels taken off her bicycle,
Of her husband's problems and successes at work
And her own special projects.
She includes a recipe for herb bread
And a web site on long leaf pines.
She ends the message
With O's and X's from the children.

I print the message,
Hold it briefly against my cheek,
Fold it gently and put it in my pocket,
Keeping it with me,
Until tomorrow
When the next e-mail will arrive.

J.J.: MENOPAUSAL

There is an angry leopard
Imprisoned within my psyche
>   Pacing
>   Stalking
From corner to corner in her confining cage.
Fed daily with my silent rage,
She devours chunks of my sanity.
Daily my leopard grows
>   Bigger
>   Stronger
>   Tougher
>   Meaner
>   Untamable
>   Unrestrainable
Resisting all civilized constraints.
Unleashed, my leopard is
>   Savage
>   Treacherous
>   Dangerous
>   Berserk—
Take heed, you irritating little jerk,
Don't you dare tease my caged leopard.

EMILY: ON THE DEATH OF SALLY, 58

Forty-eight years ago on a summer afternoon,
After church, after Sunday roast and potatoes,
Sally was waiting for me on my front porch.

Slumped on her spine in the swing,
Red-clay dusty bare feet rolling her basketball
Back and forth, back and forth,
Long, skinny, freckled legs dangling from cut off jeans,
Blackberry-stained t-shirt hanging loose,
Honey gold braids tied with red string,
Framing her square chin.

"Are you ready for me to beat you at HORSE?"
She grinned.
Of course, she did win at HORSE, again and again.
I beat her at horseshoes, or maybe she let me win.

We shared a cold watermelon,
Competitively spitting the seeds
Into the tall weeds at the edge of the back yard.

In the peach orchard we lay on our backs
In just mowed grass,
And through the green haze,
Watched Pegasus and Athena racing through the clouds.
We vowed to always be friends,
And to seal that vow,
With Sally's scout knife
We pricked out dusty big toes (thumbs were too ordinary),
Mingled our blood,
And became blood sisters, Sally and I,
On that Sunday afternoon— when we were ten.

For the rest of our yesterdays,
But none of my tomorrows,
We kept our vow of blood sisterhood, Sally and I,
That we made that June afternoon,
When we pricked our dusty big toes (thumbs were too ordinary)
In the peach orchard—
When we were ten.

ELLIE: A GARDENER'S LAMENT

The shadows lengthen,
The air cools—
It's time to put away the garden tools.
All day I've been digging in the dirt,
Sweat soaking shorts and T-shirt,
Dirt smeared and grass stained,
Muscles aching so-o-o good,
Once manicured nails now rimmed in black,
Matted hat-hair glued to my scalp,
Two water blisters on my right hand,
Lower back creaking as I stand,
Knees popping twice,
Neck burning, stinging from the sun,
The sunscreen washed off by sweat,
I welcome the rose-streaked sunset.
But, Thank God and knock on wood,
My yard sure looks good.
Over and over again,
I fight the kudzu, the weeds,
The invasive plants from once good friends,
I fight the Japanese beetles, the fire ants,
The deer, the voles, the moles, the drought.
Tomorrow, without a doubt,
I'll have to mow,
To rake, to spray, to weed,
To prune and to resow.
But, Thank God and knock on wood,
My yard sure looks good.
By plague and pestilence I am beset,
By too much dry or too much wet,
I worry and fret and call it kismet,
Have no regrets and count my assets,

And, yes!
Thank God and knock on wood,
My garden sure looks good.

ELLIE: WINTER CATALOG

Indigo,
Coreopsis,
Dianthus,
Miscanthus,
Osmanthus,
What the heck, I'll order them all.
In the woodland garden by the rock wall
I'll plant the evergreen osmanthus,
And smell its heady fragrance,
As I stroll by as twilight falls.
The indigo and golden moonbeam coreopsis
I'll plant in the butterfly border,
And let them sprawl and tangle all together.
That variegated miscanthus,
Planted behind the cerise dianthus,
I can see the way it will please,
The vertical miscanthus waving in the breeze,
With the roundly mounded dianthus
Hugging, guarding the earth,
Perfect in its berth.
Come spring and summer
They will all be blooming,
They will all be perfuming,
They will all be performing
Just as the catalog promises.
Yeah-h-h-h-

ELLIE: GREEN THUMBS

There is a garden in my hands,
        both my thumbs green,
Inherent in those hands—
        some alchemy, magic, DNA, genes,
That tell me when and where and how,
        to sow my seeds,
        to prune my vines,
        to fertilize, to mulch, to plow.

My garden is Nature's 24-Hour Diner,
Serving with a welcoming smile
        blithe swallowtails,
        bantering chickadees,
        and big-hearted bumblebees.

I am intimate with the rhythms of the earth,
        the cycles of time—
        the days, the seasons, birth and rebirth.
I scoop the soil into my hands,
        squeezing it, checking for friability, fertility,
        and slowly sift it through my fingers.
My hands now know just what this soil will grow.

My garden is Nature's Bountiful Table—
Nourishment its goal,
        of all the five senses,
        the physical whole,
        and the human soul.

ELLIE: TRANSFORMATION

When Spring arouses,
Primping and preening,
Dressing for the new season,
When the World becomes
Too potent for my senses,
The physical succumbs
To the scattering,
Randomly alighting,
Invading beads of life.

Eyes burning,
Tears trickling,
Ears itching,
Nose dripping,
Eyelids ticcing,
Sneezing—

Dizzying delights
Of chaotic order
Dismaying,
Agitating,
Bewildering,
Overwhelming—

Loving—Hating,
Anticipating—Dreading.
See-sawing,
Yo-yoing
Indicators contrary.
Living in grace and joy
In the midst
Of sneezing misery.

MARGARET: PROGRESS

My home was a southern farm home,
Built on a foundation of hard work and red Georgia clay,
Enriched by the sweat of six generations,
With land to explore and room to roam—
Woods, streams and pools, meadows and rolling hills,
Plants and wildlife thriving in their native habitats.

A neighbor died,
The Devil, disguised as a realtor,
Tempted his heirs to subdivide.
The monsters rumbled in—
Ripping, tearing, snorting,
Devouring the land, belching it out again,
Planting brick mini-mansions with three-car garages.

Another neighbor's farm,
Fertilized by millions of dollars,
Sprouted an upscale shopping mall.
A third neighbor harvested an office complex,
And a fourth reaped a regional airport with helipad.
Eminent domain split my family farm,
Followed by the incessant roar
Of traffic on newly four-laned Highway 44.

My home was a southern farm home,
With land to explore and room to roam,
Where I planned to live and die,
Before Progress pulled the horizon
To the edge of the Georgia Power lit sky.

CHRISTY: MAMA

Mama loved to cook.
Each day she fed us
Three balanced meals and two nutritious snacks,
Our favorite—her Sunday morning flapjacks.

After we kids had all moved out,
Mama loved to have us visit,
So she could feed us meals, exquisite.

Then Papa retired,
But Mama didn't.
Three meals a day plus two nutritious snacks—
For one long year, while Papa sat,
Mama did it.

On the day Mama left Papa, she left a note:
"Cook your own damn supper," in it she wrote,
And then directed him where to shove it
After he had prepared it.

Mama never cooked another meal for the rest of her life.
We all thought Mama just loved to cook;
Heck, we even thought Mama loved being Papa's wife.

SYBIL: FEMININE, FIRST PERSON, SINGULAR

During forty years of married non-bliss
I planned, shopped for, and
Prepared 42,480 meals,
Washed as many loads of laundry,
Made up as many beds,
Attended 225 PTA meetings,
Many more ball games,
And all those pets
That I never wanted,
But wound up feeding
While teaching English
To high school seniors.
Over the objections of my children
And their father,
I divorced that eternal drudgery.
Occasionally I'm a little bit sorry
I had to leave Tom to find happiness,
But, By Jove! I love living
Feminine, first person, singular!

DIANE: THE RECYCLED HOUSEWIFE

From sunup to dusk
And many hours thereafter
She fought dirt and dust
Trying to keep clean
A dusty and dirty universe.
She swept and she dusted,
She vacuumed and cursed
The eternal mess,
The endless, the mindless cleaning process.
Exhausted, she retired to her bed late at night
And dreamed of vacuuming snow in the Arctic,
Of dusting stars in the skies,
Of sweeping sand back into the Atlantic.
She died, a broom in her left hand,
A duster clutched tight in her right,
And was cremated.
Dumped from a jar,
Her ashes scattered,
Caught by the westerlies and flung afar,
Captive dust dispersed by the gusting wind.
She drifted and sifted through windows and doors
And settled on just dusted accessories,
Furniture and floors,
Where she was dusted and swept
By housewives adept
At sweeping and dusting,
At vacuuming and cursing
The dirt, the dust, the mess,
The eternal, the endless,
The mindless cleaning process.

RHEA: EARLY RETIREMENT

I was living life my way,
        Doing things when and how I wished each day—
Husband working nine to six,
        Coming home by seven,
Going to bed by eleven
        After an evening of reading and watching TV,
Golf Saturday mornings, gardening Saturday afternoons,
Sundays devoted to relaxation, marital togetherness,
        And visiting our mothers,
Seeing all we needed of each other—
Weeks, months, years marching in desirable order.

Then he torpedoed my orderly life,
        Blasting my days with irritation and strife—
Addicted to solitude,
        I could find privacy only inside my head—

I promised to love him, cleave only to him,
        For better or worse,
        In sickness and health,
        Till death do us part—
I vowed with my honor and heart—
But not one word was ever said,
No promises ever made—
        About living with him
        After he took early retirement.

JULIET: KISS AND TELL

I remember well
Andrew was the first
To kiss and tell.
I was four and
He was six years old
     when he kissed me.
I was too young to see
     the future thus foretold.

Later on there were
     Brian, Cleve, Dan, and Ed.
All kissed,
All told.
Then came Fred,
     Gene, Hal, and Ian,
Who kissed,
Who told.
By then I was getting old
     enough to see
That all the boys bragged
     after kissing me.

Then came Jack.
He kissed me;
I kissed him back.
He locked our secret kisses
     in his heart.
For me, there was no more
     powerful aphrodisiac
Than a suitor who kissed well
     but did not tell.

Submitted on 2/14/02 by Mrs. Jack (still kissing Mr. Jack)

TONI: TIMES'S CONCUBINE

She was almost as old as Time,
Was Time's Concubine,
That day when I came to dine.

We dined on what-ifs and
Supped on therefores,
Salting the past with afterwishes.

She related how happily,
When Time came courting,
She surrendered her immortality.

Then she spoke of roses,
Thorns and beauty,
Of clouds and silver linings.

When I said my manners
Ready to take my leave,
She took my hand in hers.

Holding me still and steady,
My dear, she said, Plan to die
Before you get as old as I.

MARGIE: VOLUNTEER

Dear God,
I would like to think when I come to die
That my trip through life was well spent,
That I paid my fare with my unpaid work,
A volunteer working without wages.
After all, I am my mother's heir.
She willed to me her civic pride.
"Give back. Give back," she stressed.
"Always pay for your ride."
So soon the message went around:
If you want it done, call Margie;
She won't ever let you down.
While a housewife rearing three children,
I planted trees, lobbied for cleaner air,
Served soup, tutored slow learners,
And helped get women off welfare.
I didn't waste my allotted days
Watching soap operas, playing bridge,
Or in the depths of despair.
I worked early.
I worked late.
I gave.
For too many years I worked; I gave.
And although I worked hard for your church,
I never stopped long enough to talk to you.
But, God, I'm talking to you now
Because I need to tell you I'm tired.
I'm tired of giving; I'm tired of working;
I'm tired of dragging the world around.
I've paid my fare; with your permission
I'm sitting down.
With Respect,
Margie
Amen.

GRACE: WWF

Widowed, white female,
Seventy-two and looks it,
Graying hair, wrinkles, age spots,
At least eight pounds overweight,
Financially solvent, independent,
Educated, self-sufficient,
A reader, opinionated,
Lives in the country, gardens,
Likes animals and people,
Episcopalian,
Life-long liberal Democrat,
Drink of choice— bourbon,
An environmentalist,
No children.
Looking for a companion—
To ride mules in the Grand Canyon,
Scuba dive, go to yard sales,
Fly fish, study Spanish, fly kites,
Backpack across Argentina,
With frequent stops at cantinas,
Can't be too stubborn,
MUST have grandchildren.

IRENE: A COUNTRY OF OLD WOMEN

I live in a country dry and brittle,
I live in a country of old women,
Rich old women,
Who outliving spouses, siblings,
Have inherited again and again.

Calling each other girls,
Participating in an organized whirl
Of lectures,
Socials, sing-a-longs, and outings,
We fill our days, our years.

I live in a country dry and brittle,
Hosting a citizenship of old women
Calling each other girls.
We live full lives we tell ourselves,
We live full lives we tell each other.

While year after year I wait
For The Advent of White Light
And The Ceremony at the Gate.

MYRTIS: HEAVEN

Sometimes I feel I might live forever;
At other times I know I have physical limits.
Until those physical limits are reached,
I'll go on living,
Cheerfully doing all that has to be done.

Then one day I'll bake my lemon pound cake,
And holding that cake in my left hand,
Jump right up and grab me a star with the right,
And stick my tongue out at the Devil
As I'm swinging right on over to Heaven.

I'll shake God's right hand
And then present my lemon pound cake
With my left hand, and say;
      Here I am, God.
      Now, what can I do for you?

LANA: RETROSPECT

When I am old, with shoulders bent,
Walk side to side,
And nod off at 8 p.m. watching television,
My thoughts will return to what ifs and thens—

Ill thumb the sepia photographs,
Curling at the edges in the scrapbook,
And marvel at the me that used to be,
And the you that loved me then—

Pondering how our lives would have been,
If I could have loved you then,
As much as I love the memory of you now.

KARLA AND KAREN: THE TIME OF THEIR LIVES

Shackled to her schedule,
Tethered to her time table,
Measuring life by clocks, by calendars,
Each second, minute, hour,
Day, week, month, season, year,
Minutely recorded, accounted, arranged,
Not one more minute spared than previously allotted,
But never having enough time.
Imprisoned by time as the years fly by.

Her sister, with time on her side,
Counts her minutes and hours with joy,
Measuring days by sunrise, by sunset,
Measuring months by the moon,
Years by the sun as spring follows winter,
Knowing that life is all about time,
But never having all she desires for family,
For friends, for passions, for lovers.
Yet, freed by time as the years flow by.

Bells toll the end of their ninety-year stay,
Instant, insistent—halting work, stopping play,
Tolling—You are out of time, you two,
Tolling—Eternity is waiting for you.

Interrupted, surprised, in unison they beg,
Like children being sent too early to bed,
Wait! We are just now in our prime,
Please, won't you give us a little more time.

ELIZABETH: REEL TIME

If I could enter reel time—
Fast forward action,
        previewing upcoming attractions,
Freeze frames,
        prolonging scenes of happiness and comedy,
        delaying scenes of impending tragedy,
Rewind the reel
        and begin all over again—

If I could fast forward time,
Catch flickering flashes of times prime
        waiting to delight,
        to complicate, to aggravate,
Preview future events,
        incidents, tragedies, and accidents—
Rewind time,
        selectively cutting and splicing mine—

Would I try to reconfigure fate,
        substituting XYZ for ABC,
Enter the world through a different gate,
        turning left instead of right,
Refuse to light that first cigarette,
Be more careful about sex,
        less careful about love,
Decline the role of Time's Concubine?

Would I change my story line,
Create a different plot outline,
Design new sets,
Write an alternate script of
        bumble and stumble,

complication and aggravation,
co-incident and accident,
comedy and tragedy?

ELIZABETH

.... What I want is
Bread and roses, too.

Printed in the United States
30770LVS00004B/376-423

9 781413 783216